LOIRE
gastronomique

LOIRE
gastronomique

HILAIRE WALDEN

Foreword by ANNE WILLAN

Photography by MICHELLE GARRETT

Series Editor MARIE-PIERRE MOINE

ABBEVILLE PRESS

NEW YORK   LONDON   PARIS

First published in the
United States of America
in 1993 by Abbeville Press
488 Madison Avenue
New York, NY 10022

First published in
Great Britain in 1992 by
Conran Octopus Limited
37 Shelton Street
London WC2H 9HN

ISBN 1-55859-492-2

Photographer's Researcher
and French Liaison
Sally Anne Scott
Senior Editor   Sarah Pearce
Art Editor   Alistair Plumb
Copy Editor   Lewis Esson
Editorial Assistant
Rod Mackenzie
Production   Jill Macey

*Page 1: Stained glass window at
La Châtaigneraie
Page 2: Drying wild mushrooms,
the Auvergne
Right: The characteristic flat-bottomed
boat used on the Loire river
Page 6: Fall in the Orléanais*

CONTENTS

FOREWORD

BY ANNE WILLAN

The river Loire is full of surprises. The popular image of a lazy, sunlit waterway lined with grand Renaissance palaces built for the pleasure of the kings of France is just one of the many facets of this, the longest river in France. Westward around Angers, the land flattens to the sandy, fertile soil of "the garden of France," where fruits were developed such as Beurré pears and the Reine Claude plums, named for the wife of François I. But more than 300 miles upriver, the rugged Auvergne region where the Loire rises is no garden. Here cabbage and roots are the winter staples, and cattle must be robust to survive in mountains covered with snow for a third of the year.

In between lies fine ground for growing almost every French gastronomic treat, and with the help of Michelle Garrett's evocative photographs, Hilaire Walden leads us on a connoisseur's tour of them all. With affection, she explains the history and the background of this most charismatic river. Cooks, bakers, growers, and restaurateurs come to life, and so, more importantly, do their recipes. This is a book to take into the kitchen to tackle dishes like Rabbit and Herb Terrine, Pike with Hazelnut Sauce, and Raspberry Crêpes. My own particular favorite is Chicken with Lime Blossom, a delicious combination I had not come across before (we happen to have both in our own backyard in Burgundy).

Country cooking at its best – and it is no accident that the Loire remains so rural. The river is notoriously treacherous, liable to flash floods, and full of shifting currents and sandbanks which make navigation chancy. As a result, its banks have escaped the clogging industry found along the Rhine and Rhône. Even today, environmentalists have defeated moves to dam the waters upstream, so that the Loire still flows untamed, dominating the countryside around it as it has for so many centuries. No wonder it has so much to offer in the way of fine food. And how lucky we are to have so knowledgeable a cook as Hilaire Walden to explore it for us!

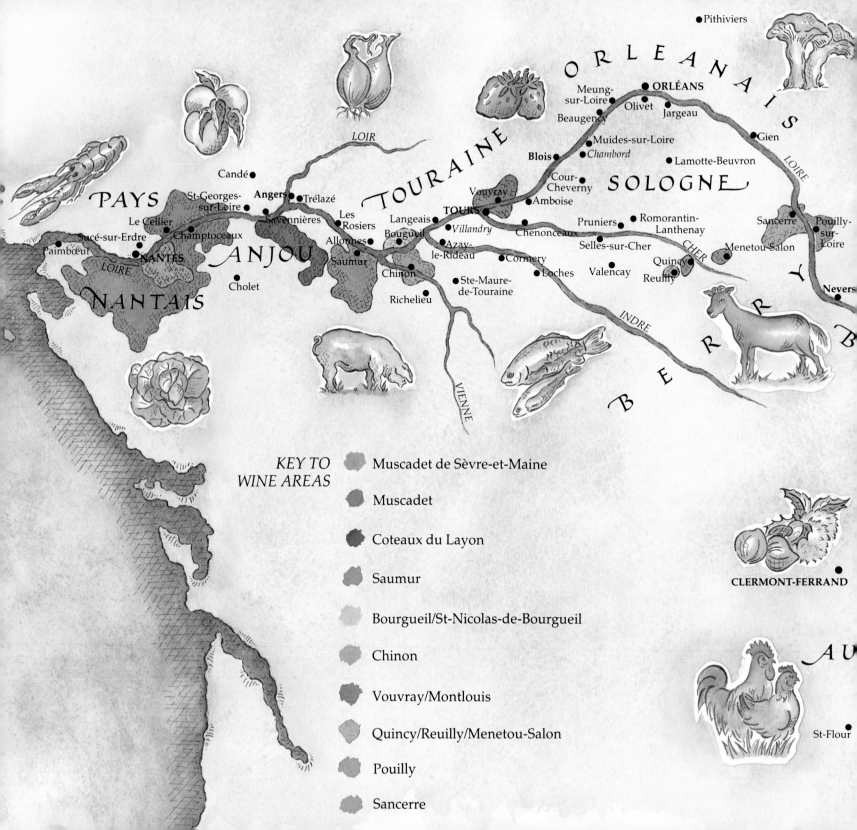

Pithiviers

ORLEANAIS

Meung-sur-Loire
ORLÉANS
Olivet
Jargeau
Beaugency
Gien

LOIR

Muides-sur-Loire
Chambord
Blois
Lamotte-Beuvron
LOIRE

Candé

TOURAINE

SOLOGNE

St-Georges-sur-Loire
Angers
Trélazé

Vouvray
Cour-Cheverny
Amboise

PAYS

Le Cellier
Savennières

Sancerre
Pouilly-sur-Loire

Sucé-sur-Erdre
Champtoceaux
Les Rosiers
Langeais
TOURS
Pruniers
Romorantin-Lanthenay

Paimbœuf
ANJOU
Bourgueil
Villandry
Chenonceaux
Menetou-Salon

NANTES
Allonnes
Azay-le-Rideau
Selles-sur-Cher
CHER

LOIRE
Saumur
Cormery
Quincy

NANTAIS
Cholet
Chinon
Loches
Valencay
Reuilly

Richelieu
Ste-Maure-de-Touraine

BERRY

Nevers

INDRE

VIENNE

BERRY

KEY TO WINE AREAS

Muscadet de Sèvre-et-Maine

Muscadet

CLERMONT-FERRAND

Coteaux du Layon

Saumur

Bourgueil/St-Nicolas-de-Bourgueil

Chinon

AU

Vouvray/Montlouis

Quincy/Reuilly/Menetou-Salon

Pouilly

St-Flour

Sancerre

INTRODUCTION

THIS BOOK IS ABOUT THE FOOD AND WINE FOUND ALONG THE LENGTH OF FRANCE'S LONGEST RIVER. DURING ITS 627-MILE JOURNEY, THE CHARACTER OF the river changes, as do the soil, countryside, and climate – and therefore the characters and ways of life of the people, along with the local foods and cooking. Great contrasts are discernible between the rocky terrain and peasant lifestyle of the Auvergne, with its rustic hearty cooking, the simple, unpretentious, homey fare of the Nivernais, Bourbonnais, and Berry, the gentle, sophisticated bourgeois cooking of Touraine, and the combination of seafood and deeply regional fare of the two staunchly individual old, cultures in Brittany and the Vendée. However, the differences happen gradually, with no abrupt changes, and many foods remain constant throughout – especially river fish, of course, although there are some subtle differences in the varieties, and wild mushrooms and game, both so beloved by the French.

The Loire rises out of a high plateau in the Auvergne, just below the rounded hump of Mont Gerbier-de-Jonc, 30 miles from Valence in the heart of the Rhône valley, and only 100 miles away from the Mediterranean. Its rivulet life begins at 4,600 feet, and the stream sets off briskly southward, toward the sun, before being diverted northwest by the massive presence of the Suc de Bauzon mountain, without which the Loire would have flowed into the Mediterranean. Instead, it forges through the cold and sparsely inhabited uplands of the eastern Auvergne, then works its way through the Loire gorge to Roanne. As it reaches the warmer, more hospitable lowlands, it gradually opens up and slows down. At Gien, the now-mature river is deflected once more, this time by the hard rocks of the Beauce, so that instead of its destiny being the Seine, it begins to describe a great arc – with Orléans at its most northerly point – and ends up heading westward.

The *fleuve royal* now flows gently, with an appropriate sedateness, through the broad fertile valley and benign climate of Touraine and Anjou, described by Flaubert, in 1847, as "varied without monotony, light, graceful, but it is a beauty which caresses without captivating, which charms without seducing, and which, in a word, has more good sense than grandeur . . ." This area was once the pleasure ground of French royalty and nobility, and it is to them that we are indebted for many of the magnificent châteaux and for turning the valley into an architectural treasury. This stretch of the Loire has also been the birthplace of many famous literary and artistic figures, such as Rabelais and Balzac, and attracted many others who have lauded its praises, from Voltaire and Leonardo da Vinci to Oscar Wilde (who described the Loire as "One of the most wonderful rivers in the world, mirroring from sea to source a hundred cities and five hundred towers.").

With the sea in sight, the Loire bisects the port of Nantes, once the capital of Brittany, then washes the southern margin of Brittany's ancient granite rock, before finally dissipating itself ignominiously into the wide estuary at the Atlantic Ocean.

The Loire used to be the backbone of life and prosperity of the lands through which it wended its way, partly because it affected the climate and influenced the drainage of the soil – for both good and bad – but also because of its importance for carrying trade. This, in turn, spawned thriving ports, businesses, and merchant classes, as well as boatmen and small hostelries to cater for them. There was even some traffic on the upper stretches, the most well-known being that of the wines taken to Orléans *en route* for Paris, but the main routes were downstream from Orléans to Nantes.

Cargoes going downstream included barrels of wine and vinegar, sacks of cereals, live fish in tanks, semiripe fruits, timber, wool, pottery, and slates from Anjou. Going upstream, there was salt, other fresh fish in tanks, and dried seafish, as well as cotton and other imports from the Americas and West Indies, such as spices, rum, and sugar.

The Loire contains almost as much solid matter as water, and islands are apt to form suddenly, then disappear just as quickly. For this reason rivermen, known variously as *nautoniers* in the fifteenth century, *bateliers* in the sixteenth, seventeenth, and eighteenth, and *mariniers* in the nineteenth, could be stuck on land at low water for long periods, and were often in danger of running aground in the shallows. A special type of boat was therefore devised for use on the Loire, with a flat bottom, a shallow draft, a raised bow, no keel or rudder, and lightweight so it could easily be moved if it did run aground (see pages 4-5).

Mississippi-style steamboats were introduced in about 1829, and increased the traffic. However, steam navigation flourished for only some 15 years. The almost simultaneous coming of the railroads made the Loire easily accessible to Paris and her lucrative markets, but dealt a fatal blow to commercial traffic on the river, which had all but disappeared by the second decade of this century.

This has, however, helped keep the Loire far cleaner than comparable rivers in other industrialized countries. This cleanliness is further helped by the dearth of industrial complexes disfiguring its banks; the many tributaries are also uncontaminated.

Along its entire journey, the Loire crosses four main wine areas: Pouilly-sur-Loire, Sancerre, and environs; Touraine; Anjou; and the Pays Nantais. In addition, there are other, lesser areas, such as St-Pourçain-sur-Sioule. Vines, mainly planted along the valley of the Loire and its tributaries such as the Cher and the Layon, cover approximately 10,000 acres and account for 11 percent of France's vineyard area for *appellation d'origine contrôlée* (AOC) and Vin de Pays wines. About three-quarters of the output of the Loire vineyards is AOC, making it France's fourth largest AOC-producing region: whites account for 43 percent of the total, reds 40 percent, rosés 12 percent, and sparkling wines 5 percent. Another 12.5 percent of the production is VDQS and 15 percent are Vin de Pays. The vineyards are divided among some 9,500 growers with an average holding of 12½ acres. In

1 *Roofscape, Auvergne.* **2** *The hills near Sancerre.* **3** *Café scene, Tours.* **4** *A goat farm at Muides-sur-Loire.* **5** *Chateau country: Saumur.* **6** *Harvesting produce for market, near Nantes.*

1	2
3	4
5	6

the Pays Nantais area, the norm is lower at 9 acres, compared with 19 acres in Anjou (the smallest area of vines that can support a family of four is calculated to be 9–10 acres).

As much as half of the wine produced comes from small growers, but in the last 10 years or so there have been considerable changes as the tradition of producing wine as part of a polyculture system is vanishing. The European Community intervention policy had meant that there was no incentive to spend effort and money in producing good wine; so quality suffered and an unfortunate amount of mediocre wine was produced. With that let-out now removed, however, and increased competition from better-quality wines from further south (as well as other countries, such as Spain and Italy, and the New World) where improvements in the standards of the wines have been made, a Loire *vigneron* has to be dedicated and knowledgeable to survive.

There are now tufts of excellence thanks to some enthusiastic *vignerons*, often well-educated and having spent some time studying oenology. They are making considerable improvements in vinification techniques and experimenting with new ideas, such as giving both red and white wines some time in new oak. Most vineyards and businesses, however, have remained small, although there is a smattering of larger companies. Some change is also due to the fact that the French are generally beginning to drink more white wine.

Because of the differing climatic and soil conditions of the regions through which the Loire flows, different grape varieties are grown and varied styles of wine produced. In general, however (and this is one of those sweeping generalizations for which exceptions are not difficult to find), Loire wines are cool, aromatic, and fresh: the whites are light to medium-bodied and crisp, ideal as aperitifs, especially during the summer months, or as accompaniments to seafood or river fish; the reds lightly fruity and enhanced by a brief sojourn in the refrigerator. The most notable exceptions are the wonderful, fragrant, sweet wines of Vouvray and the Coteaux du Layon, and some Chinon and Bourgueil, especially *vieilles vignes*, which have enough depth and complexity to make them excellent candidates for aging.

In following the course of the Loire, I have strayed as far from the river as is thought both interesting and relevant. As a convenient and generally understood shorthand, I have used names such as Touraine and Anjou, although the old provinces disappeared years ago. Because they have no official standing, boundaries are generally fairly imprecise and variable, and so open to dispute.

You can eat extremely well all along the Loire, partly because of the ready access to good-quality ingredients, particularly downstream from Orléans where the temperate climate and fertile soil result in an abundant and diverse range of excellent produce. As a testimony to the quality and variety of food in the region, in 1991, it gathered a total of over 40 Michelin stars. This does not mean that you can only eat well if you are willing to pay a lot of money. Quite the reverse: It reflects the general attitude, style, and value, and you can eat like the proverbial lord at the many excellent *fermes auberges*.

(Left)
A CORNUCOPIA OF
PRODUCE
Fruits and nuts such as these are a
common feature of the cooking in
all the areas through which the
Loire passes, because they are
harvested in the fall and can be
stored to provide both staple food
and variety during the winter.

THE YOUNG RIVER

THE LONGEST RIVER IN FRANCE STARTS ITS LIFE VERY UNPROMISINGLY AND INDISTINCTLY IN MARSHY GROUND AT THE EASTERN EDGE OF THE AUVERGNE. Remaining fairly inauspicious as it tumbles through its formative miles, not reaching true maturity until Nevers, the volcanic mountainous terrain through which it passes is, however, strikingly rugged and impressive. The landscape is interspersed with green valleys, deep rambling streams, *drailles*, or drovers' routes, some over a thousand years old, by which cattle or sheep are taken to the summer pastures, and threads of convoluted roads. As the Loire flows northward between the Bourbonnais and Nivernais, it widens and slows and the countryside becomes more gentle and open.

In the Eastern Auvergne, the prevailing character is one of unique individualism, for the remoteness of this area, the long, bitingly cold winters with only short, hot summers, the land itself, and the topography have given the peasant farmer desperately little return for his

(Left) Cockerels scratching in an Auvergnat farm.
(Above) The Loire river tumbling in its infancy through the hills of the Auvergne,
enigmatic about its future length and glory.

labor. Moreover, it is not an area conducive to industrial and commercial progress and improvement, and has consequently suffered economic stagnation and depopulation. The exodus begun in the second half of the nineteenth century has continued since, although a steady growth in tourism and leisure activities in the last 30 years has brought a more positive outlook and rekindled wily Auvergnats' natural business talent, as the many very small producers who sell their first-class homemade produce demonstrate.

For centuries, Auvergnats have had to exist on food that could be found within walking distance of their door, though the clear mountain air has been an asset as it is ideal for drying wild mushrooms (a great buy in local markets), hams, and sausages. Crops and produce must be able to grow in poor soil and survive inclement weather, so staples such as potatoes and cabbage are most common. Livestock has to be hardy and really earn its keep. Sheep can live happily on sparse uplands, and not only provide meat, but also milk both for drinking and making cheese, as well as wool for clothing; the same applies to goats. More or less every house once had at least one pig as they are both undemanding and fruitful sources of food – to coin a phrase, everything but the squeak being used – which means a cornucopia of excellent *charcuterie*, given extra variety and distinction by the hams and sausages dried in the cold mountain air.

The lushest pastures are at an average altitude of 3,300 feet, so snow comes early and disappears late, making it only possible for cattle to graze on them for 20 weeks a year. Traditionally, the cattle are driven from their winter quarters on May 24th and are brought down again on October 13th. On these days, the peace is broken by the "transhumance" of cattle, dogs, and men, and in the spring the occasion is made even more festive by the bunches of flowers tied between the horns of the cattle, or the flags attached to their bell collars. During their summer on the mountain, the herdsmen used to live in small stone houses, or *burons*, and in these they would transform the rich, flavorful cows' milk into hard cheeses to provide valuable nourishment during the winter. The system of transhumance is not popular with the majority of today's farmers, but there are still some who follow it (after all, with modern transport, they are not as marooned on the mountain as they once were), and who make cheeses, such as Fourme du Cantal *fermier*, from unpasteurized milk in the specific, traditional way that creates its special character. It is a pressed cheese molded into large cylinders; these are left to ripen 3-6 months, so the cheese is at its best in the late fall or early winter when it has developed a delicious, nutty flavor redolent of the herb-rich pastures. When making traditional *aligot* and *truffade* (see page 20), the authentic version of Cantal to use is fresh, unpressed Cantal *tomme*, because it enriches these dishes and makes them creamy rather than heavy or "cheesy."

The relatively squat Bleu d'Auvergne *fermier* was also made in the *burons* from raw summer milk and aged for 3-6 months. Although unpressed, it is firm to the touch and has a distinctive smell and flavor. Unfortunately, most Cantal and Bleu d'Auvergne are now made commercially throughout the year in modern cheese factories. Such *laitier* cheeses are made

1 *Aperitifs and liqueurs are often based on wild herbs, flowers, and medicinal plants, especially gentian and the slightly bitter vervain, which is a specialty of Le Puy.* **2** *Bleu d'Auvergne (left) and Fourme du Cantal were traditionally both made by shepherds in their burons.* **3** *A typical volcanic outcrop, a good vantage point for warding off invaders.* **4** *No good Auvergne home would be without its pigs.* **5** *Bilberry and strawberry sweets, specialties of the Auvergne.* **6** *Salers cattle were the preferred breed of the Auvergne, because they are strong, as weather-resistant as polar bears, very fertile – continuing to have calves up to an age equivalent to 80 in human terms – and give plenty of milk. Sadly, the handsome animals are a vanishing feature of the scenery.* **7** *A local fruit-studded cake made of brioche dough.* **8** *Tripoux characteristically puts to good use unlikely parts of an animal, in this case, tripe and pigs' feet.* **9** *Fresh and dried wild flowers and herbs add a distinctive nuance to the foods of the region.*

1	2	3
4	5	6
7	8	9

LENTILLES VERTES DU PUY

Particularly around Le Puy, the air of the region coupled with the volcanic soil and local microclimate are conducive to the growing, ripening, and drying of the blue-green lentils for which Le Puy has become famous in the gastronomic world. Lentils have been cultivated here for a very long

time, but just how long is a matter of dispute. One theory is that they were brought by the Moors in the eighth century, others point to a Gallo-Roman vase which was found in the old city and is believed to have contained lentils. Lentilles vertes du Puy cook so well and have such a wonderful, refined yet distinctive, flavor that the use of the name has been protected by an appellation d'origine. So strongly do the growers, who still use traditional and entirely natural methods, feel about their lentils that they have also created a trademark.

from pasteurized lowland milk, are usually only about two months old, and lack the quality and caliber of the traditional, *buron-made*, versions.

In the mountains in early spring, the ground is resplendent with a natural carpet of a host of wild flowers and fragrant herbs, which change as the year progresses: daffodils, cowslips, irises, cornflowers, purple violets with giant scented heads, and *serpolet* or wild thyme. Not only are these lovely to smell and look at, but they also provide a characteristic rich taste in the cooking of the region, giving flavor to the meat of animals that feed upon such pasture, as well as to their milk and cheese. Wild herbs and flowers are also a useful source of income: Many are carefully spread out and dried with care in the warm, dry mountain air, to be sold in the local markets or stores. They find use in *tisanes*, in cooking, and as medicines. At the Loire's first small town, Ste-Eulalie, an annual *Foire aux Violettes* is held on the Sunday following July 12th. The whole of the year's crop of violets is sold in one day to a variety of buyers, who include confectioners as well as *parfumeurs* and pharmacists.

The alluvial soil in the lower valleys is very fertile and has the ability to intensify the flavor of the produce grown in it, so there are many market gardens. In sheltered, sunny spots where it can become hot in summer, it is worthwhile planting apple and pear trees, or even plums and cherries where there is very little risk of frost; in really favored places, apricots can ripen. As the Loire flows northward, one-man market gardens grow large enough to support additional staff, and fruit trees burgeon into full-scale orchards on propitious flatter stretches.

For free, from the wild, come fish. The many clear, cold, sparkling mountain streams that tumble and chatter into the Loire are home to some fine examples. Plump, shapely, well-flavored brown trout are there for the "tickling" or catching with a line and rod, however rudimentary. To have really fresh trout cooked in a simple, sympathetic way that enhances its succulence, and dressed with a sprinkling of local walnut oil, is one of life's great eating experiences. A few crayfish are still to be found in swift-running mountain streams, if you are lucky or know where to look. There is also some farming of crayfish.

On the ground there is a wealth of game, such as the wild rabbits which become extra flavorful in the summer after they have fed on wild herbs and flowers. There are also hare, deer, and wild boar for roasting over open fires, either in the open air'or in the hearth, or reducing to melting tenderness by hours of cooking in a pot, helped along by local wine, albeit a rough one. Toward the north of the area, wild duck alight upon the lakes. In areas with grain fields, partridge may also occasionally be found.

Wander through the dappled woods in the summer, and if you are very attentive and lucky you may see, smell, and then taste delicate, delicious wild strawberries, mulberries, or even raspberries. In the Auvergne spring, which in reality is May, on the acid soils of the high shrubby heathlands where heather grows and the weather is not of the best, low, bright green bilberry bushes suddenly become speckled with small, semitransluscent green-white flowers, flushed with pink, which are replaced by blue-black fruits lightly veiled in a silvery bloom in July and August. They will be scooped off the branches with ingenious shovel-shaped implements called *peignes à myrtilles*, and made into candies and liqueurs for sale in local stores. Come the fall, there are many kinds of wild mushrooms and nuts, which in a poor, isolated area such as this have an especially important role in the diet. Chestnuts, the fruit of what is known as the "bread tree," are particularly important because they form the foundation and often the "bulk" of soups, casseroles, pies, pâtés, and stuffings, "stretching" scarce meat. The nuts could also be ground into flour for breads and batters, the leaves spread as winter feed and litter for cattle, and the wood of felled trees used for furniture or burned as charcoal.

While to us it might be gastronomic heaven to have a cache of *frais de bois* nearby, to go out in the early morning to gather a basketful of wild mushrooms for breakfast, or to have fresh wild trout for lunch, and all for free, it is of little consequence to a man who has worked hard all day in the open mountain air in all weathers, and who needs strength to do it again tomorrow, and the next day, and the next, throughout his life. Traditional dishes, therefore, had to be sustaining, economical, and easy for the housewife who had little in the way of cooking facilities to prepare and cook. Frugality was a byword, and the cooking fortifying rather than refined. Soups, of course, were a mainstay. *Soupe aux choux* and *potée auvergnate* seem to be interchangeable names for basically the same dish, although the word *potée* tends to be used more around Clermont-Ferrand and *soupe* further south. The ingredients of both can vary, but the two invariable components are pork, usually salted, and cabbage. *Potée* is likely to be a more substantial dish, containing a greater variety of vegetables, especially carrots and potatoes, along with cured sausage and, perhaps, some beef or chicken (see page 24).

Dishes such as these were prepared in huge iron pots to last a week or more, being reheated and improving as the days went by. They were usually served as two courses. First the broth would be poured over bread in a bowl, then the meat and vegetables distributed as a main course.

Bread, too, was a staple. I was told by a wiry Auvergnate who was at least 80 years old, with a knowing shake of the head, that "an empty stomach attracts illness" and "in those days" (which were anything more than 20 years ago) they relied on bread, and plenty of it, to ensure that the stomach never was. In the altitude and climate, rye was the normal grain,

DRYING MOUNTAIN HAMS

For his Jambons de Montagne, Alain Comte combines traditional "artisanal" practices with the rules of the appellation contrôlée, which govern such things as hygiene and the pigs' diet. Based on the D590 west of Le Puy at 3,300 feet above sea level (where he also sells a range of other foods), he has found his ancient old barn to be better for drying hams and sausages than a new, purpose-built shed.

Nevertheless, he is proud of his modern instruments for checking the development of the hams.

POTATOES

Potatoes are eaten extensively in the region and Auvergnats have some particularly delicious ways of cooking them.
They are often teamed with the region's delicious dairy products, as in aligot, truffade, criques, tapinaude (see page 26) and pommes de terre à la guerilla. The first of these is

probably the most famous: Over heat, cheese and cream are beaten into mashed potatoes until long ribbons are formed as the spoon is lifted. For an autumnal gratin à l'auvergnate they are mixed with an equal amount of chestnuts. Small ratte potatoes (illustrated above), with their characteristic yellow skin and firm, waxy, yellow flesh, are shaken and rolled in earthenware poêlons along with good flavorful pork fat, until crisp on the outside and tender in the center.
Potatoes are also used in farcidure, dumplings or stuffing, and to bulk out pies.

and when times were very hard, they would make do with chestnut or barley bread "as dark and tough as tree bark." A day was regularly set aside for baking, and children would hover in the kitchen, waiting for the small ball of baked dough, known as a michou, which would be given to each of them as the bread came warm from the oven. From the frequent appearance of the term in house names, such as "Notre Michou," it must still have connotations of family togetherness. An affinity with bread and baking has obviously been absorbed into the genes of many Auvergnats, because the number of people selling baked products and their general quality are both high. The more astute bakers are now publicizing the organic nature of such ingredients as rye, nuts, herbs, and cheese.

Of other baked products, the *fouasses* are exceptionally light and flavored with orange-flower water, a flavoring that can also be tasted in light brioche doughs, some of which are studded with candied fruits and baked in various crown shapes. The *pains d'épices* (see pages 41 and 57) tend to be more moist in this part of the world, and the lightest, most moist, best flavored I have ever had I consumed in some quantity near Le Puy. Although the cake was not at all oversweet, I attributed its magnificence mainly to the excellent honey to be found in the locality. As well as a wide range of wonderfully flavored honeys, the drink *hydromel* and dried pollen are also sold throughout the region.

Leaving the Auvergne, the Loire next flows between two of France's least known regions: the Nivernais on the right bank, the Bourbonnais on the left. Both are very rural with scattered populations.

Following the road along the eastern side of the Loire, the countryside of the Nivernais looks a trifle disheveled in places, and unsophisticated, although not run-down, untouched by progress. The landscape is open, with long, straight roads and fields dotted with large creamy-white cows further distinguished by long curved horns, broad muzzle, and short neck. Here is the home of Charolais cattle.

Charolais were introduced to the Nivernais in the eighteenth century and are now exported to 65 countries, the cattle being highly regarded for their lean meat and high ratio of meat to carcass. The pedigree register is kept on a computer at Nevers, and includes the physical characteristics of each animal.

To the east of the region in the Morvan hills, pigs are reared on the by-products of the dairy industry to produce succulent and flavorful Morvan hams. For this reason, ham features particularly strongly in Nivernais cooking. Most frequently it is teamed with eggs, which nearly every home would have – more or less literally – on their doorstep. For *œufs au jambon*, very thin slices of air-dried Morvan ham are fried in farm butter and then eggs broken over the top and left to cook until lightly set so that when they are broken open the yolk flows over the ham. An *omelette nivernaise* contains lightly fried ham and herbs and is cooked in the same way as a crêpe, so it is brown on both sides, and is served flat. Whole eggs in their shell may also be added to the pot along with the ham when it is being boiled, so they become impregnated with the flavor of the ham.

Across the river, the Bourbonnais is open, "easy" land with grassy plains and wooded rolling hills which, in the south, occasionally rise sufficiently to be able to claim to be mountains. Elsewhere, there are many green fields, neat hedges, the odd hedgerow tree, and low hills crowned with small woods. Around Moulins, the market town of the Bourbonnais, there are green fields, wheat fields, market gardens, and orchards. It is a well-watered landscape, with an abundance of lakes and rippling streams as well as the still pubescent Loire.

The food and cooking along this stretch of the river has the simplicity of many deeply pastoral areas in France, where people rely on products from their land and those garnered from the wild. "Potager" vegetables of onions, potatoes, and carrots, as well as lettuce and peas, produits fermiers of milk, butter, cream, and eggs, heavy bags of game from the abundant unspoiled countryside, and wild mushrooms and nuts are all used to make the straightforward "homey" dishes that form a bridge between the hearty, rustic mountain fare of the Auvergne, and the more diverse food of the Orléanais.

(Right)
VILLAGE STREET
Rural depopulation is a problem for
the Auvergne.

POTIRONÉE AUX CHÂTAIGNES

Pumpkin and Chestnut Soup

(Illustrated opposite)

In the fall, I am used to seeing the countryside lit up by splashes of vibrant orange pumpkins squatting on the ground. However, one day a sight caught my eye that caused me to get out of the car to take a closer look – pumpkin vines trained up a tree, with decorative patterns cut in the skins of the still-growing vegetables! I have also come across a pumpkin farm and a book containing 138 recipes for the humble vegetable. This recipe was given to me by the aunt of a friend and she adamantly recommended that I should use the larger *potiron* type of pumpkin and not *citrouilles*.

SERVES 5-6
¾ lb pumpkin flesh, cubed (about 3 cups)
1 cup peeled fresh chestnuts
1 large onion, chopped
2 celery stalks, chopped
2 carrots, chopped
about 1 quart good chicken stock
¼ cup milk
salt and freshly ground black pepper
crème fraîche and fresh chervil, to serve

Put the pumpkin, chestnuts, and vegetables in a large pot and pour in 3½ cups of the stock. Bring to a boil, then simmer about 30 minutes, until tender. Allow to cool slightly, then purée with the milk. Season to taste and add more stock if the soup is too thick. Return to the rinsed saucepan and reheat gently.

Serve with crème fraîche swirled in and chervil leaves scattered over the top.

CRÈME NIVERNAISE

Carrot Soup

SERVES 4
4 tbsp butter
¾ lb young carrots, chopped
white of 1 slender young leek, thinly sliced
1¼ cups vegetable stock
salt and freshly ground black pepper
1¼ cups milk
⅔ cup crème fraîche
fresh chervil leaves or chopped parsley, for garnish

Melt the butter in a heavy-based saucepan over low heat. Add the carrots and leek and cook gently, stirring occasionally, about 5-10 minutes. Add the stock and seasoning and simmer about 15 minutes or until the vegetables are tender.

Purée the vegetables and liquid, return to the pan, and add the milk and cream. Heat through without boiling.

Adjust the seasoning and serve sprinkled with chervil or parsley.

TERRINE DE LAPIN AUX HERBES

Rabbit and Herb Terrine

This is possibly the simplest of all terrines to make, and one of the lightest meat terrines I know.

SERVES 4
1 plump, young wild rabbit, dressed, skinned, and cut into small pieces
2 shallots, thinly sliced
2 tbsp chopped parsley
2-3 sprigs of fresh thyme, preferably wild
2-3 sprigs of fresh tarragon
1 fresh bay leaf
freshly ground black pepper
1½ cups white Sancerre or Pouilly-Fumé wine
large piece of pork skin, blanched
¼lb piece of mild slab bacon, thinly sliced lengthwise
about 1¼ cups rabbit or veal stock or water
extra fresh herbs, for garnish

Put the rabbit in a dish with the shallots, herbs, and pepper and pour on the wine. Cover and leave in a cool place 48 hours, turning the rabbit pieces over occasionally.

Preheat the oven to 275°F.

Line a deep baking dish with the pork skin and half of the bacon. Put in the rabbit pieces with the marinade, pressing the rabbit down well. Add sufficient boiling stock or water to cover the rabbit well, then cover with the remaining bacon. Cover the dish tightly, sealing it completely. Cook in the oven about 4½ hours, until the rabbit is very tender.

Strain off the liquid through cheese-cloth and re-cover the rabbit to keep it warm.

Remove any fat from the surface of the strained liquid, then taste and adjust the seasoning with pepper. Pour a thin layer of this liquid into a terrine or loaf pan.

Remove the bones from the rabbit, keeping the pieces of meat as large as possible. Place the pieces of rabbit and bacon in the terrine and garnish with sprigs of fresh herbs, if desired. Pour in the remaining liquid, making sure it flows completely through the pieces of meat. Cover and chill 12-24 hours.

(Right)
Pumpkin and Chestnut Soup (this page) with, in the foreground, Hare with Red Currant Jelly (page 28).

La Marmite

61 rue des Lacs
St-Flour
Tel 71 60 03 06
See recipe on this page

If it were not for a board intriguingly packed with names of local dishes, such as *potée* (illustrated below), *tripoux* (see page 16), *aligot*, and *pounti* (see opposite) standing by the doorway, La Marmite would be

easy to miss – or dismiss – because it is above a less-than-attractive bar, and approached by a not-very-inviting staircase.
The *chef-patron* is M. Mourgues, so typically Auvergnat in appearance with dark hair and a dark moustache, but atypical in his friendliness, openness, and generosity.
The promise of the board on the street is amply fulfilled, for M. Mourgues offers a range of sound, wonderfully hearty dishes on his menu, all served with no frills and no concession to gastronomic fashion.

(Above)
Made of ingredients that were once commonplace to local peasants, the omelette à l'Auvergnate made by M. Mourgues of La Marmite in St-Flour (see left) sat on my plate like an invitingly plump and yielding golden-yellow bolster. As for the taste – exploding with pure, natural, straightforward flavors – it really showed what a difference is made by using good fresh butter, fresh free-range eggs, and ham that has not been vacuum-packed or refrigerated. If only all "designer dishes" in expensive restaurants tasted as good. The other secrets of re-creating such an omelet lie in adding 1 tablespoon of cold water to the eggs while you beat them, and in seasoning the mixture with freshly ground black pepper only (no salt) before cooking.

POUNTI

Egg and Vegetable Loaf
(Illustrated opposite)

Traditional *pounti* can vary widely in solidity. Some versions have a greater proportion of flour and correspondingly less milk, while others may have more meat.
Pounti is always substantial enough for a main course, but small portions can be served as a first course or as part of a buffet. I prefer it while it is still hot or warm, but others are quite happy to eat it cold, and it is perfect for picnics.
This version is that of M. Mourgues of La Marmite in St-Flour (see left).

protection from nips), take hold of the central section of the tail, then twist and pull gently to draw out the intestine.

Putting stones in the bottom of the pot is an old trick for maintaining the temperature of the water when the fish are added, which helps to ensure their rapid dispatch.

SERVES 4
2 small carrots, chopped
2 shallots, chopped
1 leek, sliced
a bouquet garni
salt and freshly ground black pepper
about 3 cups liquid, which could be all water or fish stock, or up to 2 cups medium-bodied dry white wine substituted for the equivalent amount of water or stock
at least 10oz crayfish per person (the number will depend on their size)

Put some largish clean stones, if available, in the bottom of a large pot. Add the carrots, shallots, leek, bouquet garni, seasoning, and wine, if using, along with plenty of water (see above). Bring to a boil and simmer 20 minutes.

Add the crayfish, return the liquid to a boil quickly, and then reduce the heat. Simmer 4 minutes, or until crayfish have turned a beautiful deep carmine-pink.

Scoop out the crayfish into a large warmed bowl. Boil the cooking liquid until reduced and the flavor concentrated. Strain this over the crayfish and serve with plenty of bread to mop up the flavorful juices.

Alternatively, let the crayfish cool in the liquid, then lift them out and serve with a good, preferably homemade, mayonnaise. Reserve the liquid to use as a fish stock in another recipe.

SERVES 6
2 leeks, finely chopped
2 cups chopped green part of Swiss chard or spinach leaves
1 cabbage leaf, finely chopped
about ⅓ cup chopped parsley
¼ lb salt pork, very finely chopped
9 tbsp plain flour
4 eggs, beaten
2½ cups milk
salt and freshly ground black pepper
butter, for greasing pan

Preheat the oven to 350°F. In a bowl, mix together the vegetables, parsley, salt and pork.

Put the flour into another bowl and make a well in the center. Gradually add the eggs and milk to make a smooth batter. Season and stir into the vegetable mixture. Pour into a buttered, rectangular pan, about 9 x 11 inches in size, and bake 50-60 minutes, until just set in the center.

ÉCREVISSES À LA NAGE

Crayfish in an Aromatic Broth

If you are lucky enough to find some wild crayfish, remove the black thread of intestine running down their backs: Hold the fish firmly with your free hand (it is a very good idea to wear rubber gloves for

minutes; keep an eye on the potatoes to make sure that they do not stick to the bottom of the pan.

Preheat the oven to about 350°F, or preheat the broiler.

Transfer the contents of the saucepan to a gratin or flameproof dish, pour on the remaining crème fraîche, and sprinkle with the cheese. Place in the oven or under the broiler about 5-10 minutes, until the cheese is melted and golden.

LENTILLES VERTES DU PUY

Green Puy Lentils in the Auvergne Style

This is the basic recipe for lentils, to which can be added chunky country-style sausages, or raw ham in cubes or as a small piece, to make a typically Auvergnat dish – trencherman fare but based on good ingredients and full of flavor.

SERVES 4
¼lb piece of salt pork or slab bacon, cut across into strips
1 onion, finely chopped
1 carrot, finely chopped
1 leek, sliced
1⅓ cups Puy lentils (see page 18)
2¼ cups veal stock or water
a fresh bouquet garni consisting of a large sprig of thyme, 1 bay leaf, 3 sprigs of parsley, and a small sprig of rosemary
salt and freshly ground black pepper

Heat the pork or bacon in a Dutch oven, stirring occasionally, until the fat runs.

Add the vegetables and cook, stirring occasionally, about 3 minutes without allowing them to color. Stir in the lentils. After a few seconds, add the stock or

TAPINAUDE

Creamy Potatoes with Cheese
(Illustrated above)

There are many recipes for this dish, but this one is an authentic old version used by M. Dray of La Renaissance (see opposite). It is less rich than some because it is made from half milk and half cream – which nearly replicates traditional creamy farmhouse milk – and does not include eggs, as in those versions in which the potatoes are baked in a custard. Cooking the potato in the sauce seems to produce a result that is "creamy" enough in itself. M. Dray serves *tapinaude* with simple main courses, but it can also be served as a first course, or as a light lunch or supper dish.

SERVES 4
2 tbsp unsalted butter, plus more for greasing
2½ tsp plain flour
1¼ cups milk
1¼ cups crème fraîche
salt and freshly ground black pepper
1½lb potatoes, peeled and thinly sliced
1 cup shredded Cantal or Gruyère cheese

Melt the butter in a saucepan, then stir in the flour. Over very low heat, gradually stir in the milk and three-quarters of the crème fraîche, keeping the mixture smooth. Bring to a boil, stirring, and simmer 5 minutes. Season.

Rinse the potato slices and drain well. Place them in a saucepan, pour in the sauce, and bring to a boil, stirring. Cover with buttered parchment paper and then the saucepan lid and cook gently about 30

water with the bouquet garni. Bring to a boil, then simmer gently about 20 minutes or until the lentils are tender.

Discard the bouquet garni and adjust the seasoning with salt and pepper to taste. Serve at once.

COQ AU VIN

Chicken in Red Wine

Slowly cooking a tough male bird in red wine to make it tender is so obvious that it must have been practiced in many other parts of France, but I don't know of an area that can lay claim to such a good tale about the creation of the dish. The story is that during the Roman invasion of the Auvergne, the Gauls were forced to retreat to the slopes of the Puy de Dôme where they were besieged by Caesar's troops. So far, this is true. One day the Gallic chief, symbolically thumbing his nose at Caesar, sent him an old, dried-up cockerel. Caesar decided that the insult could be turned to his advantage. He declared a truce and invited the Gallic chief to a dinner *à deux*. A wonderfully flavored dish with a rich sauce was served, and the Gaul realized that his tough old cockerel, cooked long and slowly in the local wine by Caesar's chefs, had been transformed into a culinary masterpiece.

The nearest you will probably be able to get to a tough old cockerel is a stewing chicken; failing that, use a large free-range chicken. You can marinate it in the wine overnight for a gamy flavor, but this will not much improve the tenderness.

This is a country recipe intended for good eating only – no mushrooms and bacon scattered artfully on top, nor croutons around the edge.

SERVES 4

2 tbsp unsalted butter
¼lb slab bacon, cut across into strips
4½lb chicken, any surplus fat removed from the cavity and cut into pieces
18-20 small white onions
1 carrot, chopped
½lb mushrooms, preferably fresh wild ones or cultivated brown mushrooms
2 cups red wine
a large bouquet garni of fresh herbs, including thyme, bay leaf, parsley, tarragon, and a little rosemary
salt and freshly ground black pepper
chopped parsley, for garnish

Heat the butter in a Dutch oven, add the bacon, and fry until the fat runs. Remove and drain on a paper towel. Put in the chicken pieces, skin-side down, and cook over medium heat until golden. Transfer to paper towels to drain.

Add the onions and carrot to the pot and cook until lightly browned, then transfer to paper towels. Add the mushrooms and cook, stirring, 2-3 minutes.

Remove the mushrooms and pour the fat from the pot. Stir the wine into the sediments in the pot, return the onions and carrot, and bring to a boil. Skim off any fat, lower the heat slightly, and add the chicken, bouquet garni, and seasoning. Add water or stock if the chicken is not covered. Adjust the heat so the liquid is barely moving, cover tightly, and cook very gently for about 1 hour, until the chicken is very tender, adding the mushrooms for the last 10 minutes or so.

Transfer the chicken and vegetables to a warmed dish and keep warm. Boil the cooking liquid until well reduced. Adjust the seasoning and remove the bouquet garni. Return the chicken and vegetables to the sauce, garnish, and serve.

LA RENAISSANCE **
Magny-Cours
nr Nevers
Tel 86 58 10 40
See recipe far left

Chef-patron Jean-Claude Dray has been cooking with old-fashioned generosity at La

Renaissance over 30 years. Born in Nevers, he takes great pleasure in using local products and researching old regional recipes. He then incorporates both into his repertoire, where they sit quite happily alongside dishes befitting a Michelin two-star restaurant.

Behind the restaurant is a large garden where M. Dray and a gardener between them grow nearly half of all the vegetables and herbs used in the restaurant.

Plucking a leaf here, a sprig there, he showed me with great pride his especially selected varieties, such as the watercress that does not have to have its feet in water and which tastes milder and sweeter than usual.

BŒUF AUX HERBES

Beef and Vegetable Stew

At the beginning of the spring "trans-humance" (see page 17), a cow would be chosen from the herd, her horns adorned with an extra-special garland, and she would be allowed to graze in whichever pastures she fancied until Midsummer's Day, June 24. Her halcyon days were then over—her destiny to be simmered slowly in a large pot with plenty of wild mountain herbs and fresh early-summer vegetables to provide a feast for the villagers.

SERVES 4-6
¼lb unsmoked slab bacon, cut across into
thin strips
2½lb boneless brisket of beef, cut into large cubes
2 cups dry white wine
a bouquet garni
salt and freshly ground black pepper
8 baby carrots
4-6 baby turnips
3 small heads of lettuce or lettuce hearts
5oz small onions or shallots
1 cup shelled green peas

Cook the bacon in a Dutch oven over low heat until the fat runs. Increase the heat, add the beef, and brown.

In a saucepan, bring the wine to a boil with the bouquet garni. Pour this into the pot, season, and add water just to cover the beef. Bring to a simmer, cover tightly and cook gently for about 2 hours.

Meanwhile, blanch the carrots and turnips 5 minutes in boiling salted water. Drain. Blanch the lettuce 2 minutes, drain well, and cut into quarters.

Stir the carrots, turnips, and onions into the pot, adding more water if necessary. Cover and cook 10 minutes. Add the peas and lettuce, cover, and cook 10 minutes longer, or until the vegetables are tender.

Check the seasoning and concentration of the cooking liquor: If it is too weak, transfer the meat and vegetables to a warmed dish and boil the liquid until reduced sufficiently. Return the meat and vegetables to the pot to serve.

FETCHOULETTE

Kid with Sorrel

In the spring, with only the odd lucky exception that will be kept for breeding, the young male goats are culled (in a culture where the *raison d'être* of animals is as food, they serve no other useful purpose). At this age they have none of the pungent "goatiness" associated with older animals, but are delicately flavored and tender. Breast of lamb or veal also work well in this dish if kid is unavailable.

SERVES 4
2 tbsp butter
¼lb unsmoked slab bacon, cut across into
thin strips
1½lb boneless breast of kid, cut into cubes
1 tbsp flour
1 cup dry white wine
a fresh bouquet garni consisting of a bay leaf, 2
sprigs of thyme, and 2 sprigs of parsley
a large bunch of young sorrel, trimmed and torn
into shreds
salt and freshly ground black pepper

Melt half of the butter in a Dutch oven, add the meat, and brown over medium heat, stirring occasionally.

Reduce the heat, sprinkle with the flour, and cook 2-3 minutes longer. Stir in the wine and add sufficient water to cover. Add the bouquet garni and bring just to a simmer. Cover and cook very gently about 40 minutes, stirring occasionally, until the kid is tender.

Meanwhile, gently cook the sorrel in the remaining butter 2-3 minutes. Add to the pot, and continue to cook, uncovered, for about 10 minutes. Season and serve.

LIÈVRE À LA DUCHAMBAIS

Hare with Red Currant Jelly
(Illustrated on page 23)

SERVES 2
1 saddle of hare
2 shallots, finely chopped
about 1¼ cups crème fraîche
2 tbsp white wine vinegar
salt and freshly ground black pepper
1 tbsp red currant jelly

Preheat the oven to 275°F.

Make sure the thin, silvery membrane which covers the saddle closely has been removed. Put the saddle into a Dutch oven or heavy casserole that it just fits. Scatter the shallots over the hare. Stir together the crème fraîche, vinegar, and seasoning and pour over the hare; it should just be covered. Cover tightly and cook in the oven until tender, 1-1½ hours.

Lift the hare from the pot, allowing excess sauce to drain off. Place the saddle on a warmed plate and keep warm.

Pour the sauce, which will look unattractively curdled, into a small saucepan. Stir in the red currant jelly and boil hard until smooth, reduced, and thickened. Season and stir in any hare juices.

Carve the saddle, including the fillet that is underneath, lengthwise into thin slices. Serve with the sauce.

CONFITURE DE MARRONS

Chestnut Conserve

(Illustrated below)

In France, this would be served with crème fraîche and thin cookies for dessert.

MAKES ABOUT 2¾lb
2¼lb chestnuts
2¼ cups sugar
1 vanilla bean

With the point of a sharp knife, make an incision around the top of each chestnut. Drop them into boiling water and blanch 5 minutes. Drain and let cool a little, then peel them.

Put the peeled chestnuts into a saucepan and add just enough water to cover. Cover the pan, bring to a boil, and simmer about 30 minutes.

Meanwhile, put the sugar into a small heavy-based saucepan with ½ cup of water. Split the vanilla bean lengthwise and remove the seeds. Add both the bean and seeds to the sugar and heat gently until all the sugar has dissolved, then boil about 15 minutes.

Drain the chestnuts, reserving the cooking liquid, then purée them. Add enough water to the reserved liquid to make 2¼ cups and blend this into the purée. Stir this mixture into the syrup and boil about 10 minutes, stirring constantly.

Pour into warm, dry, sterilized jars or pots and cover tightly.

INTO THE VAL-DE-LOIRE

PAST BERRY TO THE SOLOGNE AND THE ORLÉANAIS

CONTINUING ITS JOURNEY NORTHWARD TO ORLÉANS, THE LOIRE FLOWS PAST BERRY, HOME OF CROTTINS DE CHAVIGNOL CHEESE, AND THE VINEYARDS OF Sancerre with its twin wine Pouilly-Fumé across the river. Pouilly-sur-Loire is really just inside the last straggling outskirts of the Nivernais (see previous chapter), before it and the Berry merge imperceptibly into the Orléanais, with its *pains d'épices*, historic saffron, and some of the best vinegar in the world.

The city of Orléans, on the northern bank of the Loire, sits at the point where the river is deflected westward, forming a wide loop running through rich, fertile soil surrounded by beautiful forests. Stretching into the Touraine south of the river, to the west of Berry and thus contained in this loop, lies the Sologne, country of *tarte Tatin*, superb asparagus, and *confréries* by the dozen.

(Opposite) The Sologne is encased within the bend of the Loire. It is a little-known region with a distinct character and plenty to interest the food lover, especially during the fall and winter when game and wild mushrooms are in season.
(Above) There is some riding to hounds in the Sologne. The dogs at Château de Cheverny are a crossbreed of English hound for sturdiness, and Poitevin for "nose."

32 Into the Val-de-Loire

1 Neat stack of wood. **2** The restaurant at *Auberge des Templiers, Les Bézards.* **3** Stained-glass window at *Château de Cheverny*, where there is also a hunting museum; in one room around 200 pairs of antlers from slaughtered stags are displayed. **4** The flat-bottomed Loire boats, known as chalands or gabares. **5** *Collecting fishing bait from the river.* **6** *Walnuts.* **7** Hunters with guns and dogs. **8** Cotignac is a quince paste or jelly well worth bringing home for yourself or as a gift, as it is (or should be) wonderfully flavored with the powerful fragrance of the fruit. Many commercially made cotignacs dilute the quinces with apples, so check the label before buying. Sometimes cut into shapes and rolled in sugar, cotignac is also sold set in round containers.
 9 *A country garden near Beaugency.* **10** Gâteau de Pithiviers feuilletté *(see page 57).* **11** Milk churns at a goat-cheese maker near Muides-sur-Loire; goats produce less milk than cows. **12** Romorantin-Lanthenay, the market town of the Sologne. **13** Cerises d'Olivet were once a local specialty.

1	2	3	4	
5	6	7	8	9
	10	11	12	13

ASPARAGUS

Asparagus is an important crop in a number of areas of the Sologne, chiefly centered around Contres and Soings-en-Sologne. But you will never actually see the prized vegetable growing because the thick-stemmed white asparagus is invariably cultivated so that it does not see the light of day. Harvesting is effected with a special tool looking like a carpenter's gouge. The pickers run this implement into the earth with

astonishing dexterity, probing for the asparagus stalk. The tool is then slid down the stalk, with the asparagus cradled in its convex side, and the stalk is cut off cleanly at the bottom with a deft slight twist of the wrist.

(Opposite)
CHÂTEAU DE CHEVERNY

The Sologne, labeled "redoubtable" by many, is not homogeneous, and is often unjustly dismissed in its entirety as dreary and inhospitable. Much of the area was once a fine oak forest, but indiscriminate deforestation in the Middle Ages reduced it to a sour wilderness, rather than the hoped-for arable land. Big trees are water pumps, and an acre of adult broad-leaved trees will normally pump thousands of gallons of water a day out of the soil. If virtually all the trees are removed without provision for drainage, the soil will become water-logged. This is especially true in an area such as the Sologne, where there is surface clay, a damp climate, and an accumulation of water from the Massif Central. As a result of deforestation here, a survey, in 1518, estimated there to be over 4,000 lakes, and reclaiming the land with hardwood forest proved impossible. Little success also resulted from other initiatives, such as that by Napoléon II in the mid-nineteenth century to construct many drainage channels, including the Canal de la Sauldre. Recent plantations of pine trees have been more successful in the job of reclamation, but these have done nothing for the landscape and have probably contributed to the unwelcoming image of the Sologne.

Physically, spiritually, and temperamentally the Sologne is quite different from its neighbors – especially those further down the Loire – but it is not at all monotonous. True, in the east there are some uninspiring pine forests, but there is a fair bit of heathland, with a quiet, away-from-it-all openness that does have a certain beauty; it takes on a softer character when covered with sunny yellow broom, purple heather, and ling.

What population the Sologne has is scattered in small villages and towns, many of which are interesting if isolated. With a frugal livelihood, the region has suffered from depopulation, although it is not as poor now as it once was.

In the western half of the region, where the soil is dry, horticulture is an important activity. Small, enthusiastic producers are realizing the potential for a modest living from growing specialist fruit and vegetables, with asparagus and strawberries as the most lucrative.

Some of the finest asparagus in France is grown in the Sologne. It was first planted in the 1870s by a local man, Charles Depezay. He had been garrisoned near Argenteuil, northwest of Paris, and had spent long hours crouched in sandy fields where asparagus flourished. Noticing that the soil closely resembled that at home, he took some plants back with him. Now it is an established and important crop, and one or two growers are even experimenting with green varieties, which traditionally the French have eschewed.

The Sologne is rich with culinary delights, for there are plenty of good, natural ingredients and artisan producers who are all apparently flourishing. They are proud of their craft and their products and not simply jumping on the nostalgia bandwagon using "olde-worlde" packaging. Driving through the region is a heavenly experience for food lovers because there is plenty of evidence of small farms producing natural *produits fermiers*. As well as products such as milk, cream, eggs, and goat cheese, these include duck (which is invariably turned into *confit*), goose (of which nearly every imaginable part is used: gizzards, neck, hearts, and livers for *foie gras*), poultry and guinea fowl, and *rillettes* and other cooked

EAU-DE-VIE DE POIRE WILLIAMS

The most interesting tipples of the Orléanais, eaux-de-vie are produced from the orchards south of the city by the cooperative Covifruit. Pear is the most important, with 5–600 metric tons of Poires Williams being distilled annually between September and November and during January. The production of a quart of their 50% alcohol eau-de-vie

(10% higher than most others) requires over 2 pounds of pears. To produce the eau-de-vie with a pear in the bottle, special wide-shouldered bottles are slipped over the fruit while it is still growing on the trees in about May or June. Once mature, they are cut from the trees and the space in the bottles filled with neutral alcohol. This is replaced by pear eau-de-vie just prior to shipping.

(Above right)
QUIET SOLOGNE FARM

dishes. These are either sold from the producers' own premises or in stores in many of the local villages and towns, such as Jargeau, celebrated for the fine quality of its sausages and the other products to be found in its *charcuteries* (the Grand rue, or rue Gambetta, is well worth a detour for the number and quality of its food stores).

In Romorantin-Lanthenay, the capital of the Sologne, the annual *Journées Gastronomiques* are staged over the last weekend of October. Traffic is banished from the town and a public-address system festooning the streets keeps everyone informed of events in the three marquees where culinary competitions are held and hundreds of small producers exhibit, offering their products for tasting (fortunately there are not many wine-makers). The quality of the products is so high, it has led to the establishment of a nationally known label of the collective trademark of the *Journées Gastronomiques de Sologne*. The region's innumerable *confréries* have a presence at the *Journées*, ranging from the "Confrérie de Pâte de Citrouille" for those with an interest in pumpkins, to the "Confrérie de Tastandouillettes de Menn'tou-sur-Cher" representing local sausage lovers, and the "Confrérie de Mousses des Mangeux de Grenouilles" consisting of the many devoted aficionados of frogs' legs.

Because of the poor soil there are generally few cattle, although there is some grazing near the region's edges. Sheep are also rare, although in Fontaines-en-Sologne some of the old compact Solognote breed are reared; they are renowned for the flavor and texture of their meat. The region does boast a diverse selection of good *charcuterie*: fat, juicy *boudins noirs* with cream and onions, with Gamay, or even with wild mushrooms. *Boudins noirs* with chestnuts are a specialty of the village of Pruniers-en-Sologne, near Romorantin. There are also *boudins blancs Solognots*, *saucissons secs* and dried hams of wild boar, venison *saucissons* and *saucissons secs*, *rillettes* of wild rabbit, and *rillons*.

Hunting, both on horseback and on foot with guns, is a favorite pastime and a good source of revenue because successful Parisian businessmen will pay large sums to take part in organized "hospitality" shoots held at the hunting lodges where once the aristocracy gathered. Pheasants, deer, and "wild" boar are reared on farms and released just before these shoots, but some true wild game may still be found, especially rabbits and duck. Even so, during the fall and winter, game is the local restaurants' staple.

The many lakes, rivers, lazy canals, streams, gleaming ponds, and *étangs* are a fisherman's paradise. They are increasingly used as a source of income, with *"élevage"* (rearing) of carp, trout, and pike. Other catches include tench, gudgeon, barbel, and bleak, and in winter eels make easy pickings when they cluster around the gates as the *étangs* are drained.

Honey from bees that have roamed the heathlands and pine forests is used in many of the local sweetmeats, such as *ruches de Salbris* (honey-glazed cookies), *croquets Solognots* (almond cookies), and a wonderful, tender, moist honey-and-pumpkin bread, made by Lebrun's in Romorantin, containing succulent, tangy pieces of citron peel.

Other products to be found in *boulangeries* and *pâtisseries* include *galettes de pommes de terre* (see page 46) and *pâtes de pommes de terre*, which are made from mashed potatoes and *fromage blanc* mixed with flour to make a dough that is then rolled and folded three or four times, as in the making of puff pastry. *Pâte de fromage* is made in a similar way, replacing the potato with soft goat cheese which is about two weeks old. *Bourprudinier* or *briprunelloise* are very long savory pastries filled with prized Prudiniers sausages. *Boudins de Prudinier aux pommes feuilletées* have potato incorporated into the pastry, and the same filling is used for *fridules*, puff pastry triangles. *Pain sur Boulenc* is bread made by an *artisan boulanger* in the old-fashioned way using pure, natural ingredients, *boules aux châtaignes* are rolls with chestnuts, and *pain de fromage* contains pieces of cheese mixed into the bread dough.

However, the Sologne's best-known pastry is the famous caramelized upside-down apple tart known as *tarte des demoiselles Tatin*. This is reputed to have first been made in the small town of Lamotte-Beuvron by the *sœurs Tatin*, who were local hoteliers. The sisters moved from the hotel in 1907, but it thrives today as the Hôtel Tatin, 5 ave de Vierzon, capitalizing on the name and the legend. The sisters' coal- and wood-burning, blue-tiled stove survives, but the present *chef-patron*, Gilles Caillé, who bought the hotel in 1968, uses a conventional gas oven to bake ten or so tarts a day. He is a member of

TARTE TATIN

During the 1850s, two sisters, Stéphanie (Fanny) and Caroline, moved from a nearby village to Lamotte-Beuvron and built the sturdy stucco-fronted Hôtel-Terminus Tatin to cater for visiting hunters and travelers. According to a version of the legend, one day Caroline inadvertently put the apples she had cooked in butter and sugar for a tart into a pastryless pie

pan. Rather than tipping out the mixture so she could line the pan with pastry in the normal way, she placed the pastry over the apples and then inverted the pie after baking it to make a tarte renversée.

Another version simply says that such tartes renversées had been made throughout France for years, but the Tatin sisters' recipe "caught on" and became famous. The celebrated gastronome Curnonsky (see page 105) even came down from Paris by train to try the famous tarte Tatin, but his verdict is not recorded.

La Confrérie des Lichonneaux de Tarte Tatin, and so makes his tarts according to the club's rules. *Pâte sucrée*, not puff pastry, is used, and the apples, butter, and sugar are not caramelized on top of the stove before baking (see page 56).

Flowing north to Orléans, the Loire passes through land that has been a center for the experimental cultivation of fruit and vegetables since the Middle Ages. In and around Olivet, right in the suburbs of Orléans, there still flourish small orchards and market gardens growing apples, especially Golden Delicious and Granny Smith, but also some reinettes, and some old specialties of cherries and pears (Beurré Hardy and Bon Chrétien, so appreciated by Marcel Proust, have virtually disappeared but Bartletts remain). Sadly, with the temptation of high prices for the land for building, the acreage devoted to market gardening can only be expected to decline.

Here a still not-infrequent sight in sunny open places, or sheltering against a garden wall, are the crooked branches and dark green leaves of quince trees. In April and May, they are at their prettiest, decked with white or rose-pink blossoms, from late September, the leaves turn to bright autumnal tints, and the downy golden fruits develop their powerful and unmistakable rich fragrance. The quinces are picked when they are golden, although they will still feel firm and will be too hard to eat raw. In fact, they are not particularly pleasant when raw, but when cooked they soften and release their heavenly, luscious, honey-like flavor and aroma (see the recipe for Wild Duck with Quince on page 55).

Quinces are popular in tarts and are used to flavor *eaux-de-vie*. However, they are most usually associated with preserves, such as the lovely *gelée de coing* and the more coarsely textured *marmelade de coing*. Cotignac (see page 33) is a thick quince paste which can be cut into cubes or lozenge shapes and rolled in sugar, similar to *pâte des fruits*. Commercially, the quince is invariably mixed with apples and this adulteration may also be practiced domestically, apples being more widely available and easier to handle.

Orléans is at the most northerly point on the Loire, and grew because of its proximity to the lucrative markets of Paris and its environs as well as its position at a crossroads between north and south, east and west; it made a natural loading point for produce going up and down the river. From the Middle Ages, Orléans was a very important grain market and boat-building center, and when supplies of sugar cane started coming from the West Indies, many refineries sprang up giving rise to several sweet specialties, such as the *bonblancs* that used to be sold by street sellers crying "*des bonblancs, tout chaud blancs . . . ces bonblancs.*"

Orléans also held an important position in the wine trade, being at the spot where cargoes of wine were unloaded for despatch by road to Paris. By the time wine reached Orléans, especially from upstream, much had often turned to vinegar, so an enterprising soul hit on the idea of using what would otherwise be wasted. By 1392, such was the reputation of the town's vinegar that it was recognized as a vinegar-making center by Charles VI, and, in 1580, Henri III created the Guild of Master Vinegar-Makers by letters patent.

The special, gentle process used to make *vinaigre d'Orléans* (which is now protected by an *appellation contrôlée*) was developed in 1797 by a M. Pouret and a M. Martin (see right). The two joined forces in 1841 to establish Martin-Pouret, now the sole surviving company making Orléans vinegar, as opposed to making vinegar in Orléans. Unlike its forebears, the company does not nowadays buy in wine that has turned to vinegar, but instead uses wine that is surplus to production – and this only after it has been tasted by the company experts to make sure that it has a good flavor. About 60–70 percent of the wine comes from the Loire, the rest from the classic wine-making areas such as Bordeaux, Burgundy, and Beaujolais.

North of the city are the rich, rolling, poppy-speckled grain lands of the Beauce and the Gâtinais, where larks soar invisibly into the wide, wide horizon, their merry song being the only indication of their presence. In the midst of the seemingly boundless fields snuggles the small town of Pithiviers, where there is a long tradition of baking – hardly surprising considering the surrounding abundant crops.

If local legend is to be believed, *pain d'épices* has been a specialty of Pithiviers since the end of the tenth century. About 992, an Armenian bishop, Gregory, began living as a hermit in a cave about 1¼ miles from the town. In 999, he realized he was dying and invited priests, ministers, and secular pious people to visit him. To refresh their souls after the journey, he offered canticles and hymns, but for their bodies he offered a spiced Armenian honey cake. As his guests tasted this, they thought they were enjoying the "delights of Paradise"; and so was born the fame of the town's *pain d'épices*.

VINAIGRE D'ORLÉANS
Jean-François Martin, great-grandson of the original M. Martin, explained to me during our tour of his premises on the outskirts of Orléans that the vinegar process starts with the blending of the various wines to ensure a consistent base; then the wine is left in oak *vaisseaux*, or barrels, some of which are over 100 years old. Each barrel contains one part air and two parts wine/vinegar and the

procedure used is similar to the sherry *solera* system in that the barrels are never emptied; about half of the wine/vinegar is pumped off and replaced by new wine. The barrels are placed on oak shelving in dark, temperature-controlled rooms to allow fermentation to take place. When there is no more alcohol, the vinegar is aged six months to reduce the acidity and develop the aroma and bouquet.

(Opposite)
BOAT HOUSE NEAR OLIVET

(Opposite)
THE WHEATFIELDS OF THE BEAUCE
North of Orléans lie the productive agricultural lands of the Beauce. Unfortunately, due to the use of chemical sprays the welcoming, nostalgic sight of gay, red poppies adding splashes of contrasting color to the yellow, undulating sea of wheat is one almost of the past.

(Left)
PAIN D'ÉPICES
The small town of Pithiviers, north of Orléans, is so famed for its two eponymous gâteaux that many do not realize that it has a third specialty, pain d'épices, a honey and spice cake
(see page 57).

Most modern *pains d'épices* are rather dry and generally considered everyday food "*pour les enfants*," certainly not a prominent specialty in the numerous *pâtisseries*. In these establishments, pride of place is given to two eponymous gâteaux: One is a double-crust, almond-filled, free-form puff pastry pie, with a distinctive swirl pattern on top (see pages 32 and 57); the other is a brioche-type dough studded with crystallized or candied fruits and decorated with icing. There is also *pâté d'alouette* which should now be but a legend, because lark shooting was legally banned in 1982, but stores still claim to sell it (although how much lark is actually in their pies is debatable) and local people definitely do still make it at home.

In the Gâtinais, saffron was cultivated from the Middle Ages. The area became the world's center for saffron production, and whole families, even whole villages, were involved in growing the purple fall-flowering *Crocus sativus*. At its height, annual output equaled that of the world today, about 60 metric tons. The Musée du Safran, in the tiny sleepy town of Boynes, displays artefacts such as a cloth sack of saffron dated 1772, and the trays in which the fine stamens (which had to be removed from each crocus by hand) were suspended over a fire to dry. What a wonderful aroma must have pervaded the vicinity at harvest time!

CHEESE

The famous Crottin de Chavignol is made from the milk of the goats of eastern Berry, around Sancerre. Mention goat cheese to many people and the image conjured up will bear some resemblance to Crottin de Chavignol – small, usually hard, smelly, and strong – and probably produce a turning up of the nose. At one time this reaction was perhaps justified because, until given the protection of an *appellation d'origine*, there were some poorly made, not very pleasant specimens masquerading as "Crottins de Chavignol." Now, however, the absence of the official seal reveals an interloper.

Chavignol cheese has a very long history, and similar cheeses have been made by local peasants since the sixteenth century. However, the name "crottin" was not used until 1829, and supposedly resulted from the resemblance of the blackened mature Chavignol cheese to a small oil lamp with that name. Traditionally, a Sancerrois farm worker would take a few hard *crottins* with him to the fields to nibble during the day.

There are many small producers of goat cheese and some *fromage de brebis* producers in the Sologne. In the Orléanais, however, cows' milk is used for cheeses such as Olivet. There are four types of Olivet, all smallish disks. Simple Olivet is similar to Coulommiers, rich and supple in texture with a light, faintly sweet flavor and smooth, pale-yellow paste. Olivet *au foin* is a naturally made cheese which has been ripened in hay and wrapped in hay or leaves. Occasionally it is eaten fresh, or

(Above)
GOAT FARM
Many small farmers have just a few of the brown Alpine breed of goat, which they keep for milk for cheese.

(Right)
OLIVET CHEESE
The small town of Olivet is today virtually a suburb of Orléans, so it seems strange that it should be the home of a cheese, and that the cheese should be one of the few made from cows' milk that are found along the whole of the Loire.

after half-ripening, that is just 10–14 days. Olivet bleu is actually not a blue-veined cheese, but a smooth, straw-yellow cheese with a rich, supple texture and a natural blueish tinge to its quite bloomy rind, acquired during a month's curing in local chalk caves. It has a mildly fruity flavor which can sometimes be sharp. The best time for eating it is from spring to the end of the fall. Olivet *cendré* is ripened in ash-filled casks for about three months so that its flavor deepens and becomes more savory. This aging time means it is available into the winter. Originally it was made when milk was plentiful, to preserve it for times of low milk yields or for when there was a demand for "picnic" foods to take to the fields, as at haymaking and harvest time. Other Orléanais cows' milk cheeses include: Bondaroy *au foin*, a soft cheese with a tangy flavor which is cured in hay for five weeks; Frinault, a small richly flavored disk of full-fat cows' milk cheese; Frinault *cendré*, and St-Benoit, or St-Benoist, a farm-made disk of part-skim milk cheese with a pale rind and fruity flavor.

WINES

The best-known wine of this whole area, white Sancerre, is produced in Berry. Because of the similarities to – and frequent association with – Pouilly-Fumé, which is made just across the river, I am going to cover the two together, although strictly speaking Pouilly-Fumé comes from the *département* of Nivernais.

Both Pouilly-Fumé and white Sancerre are made from the same grape variety, sauvignon, which gives them their pale green/yellow color, their slightly smoky/musky/grassy bouquet, and a flavor vibrant with crisp, lively, fruity tones, redolent of black currant leaves and ripe gooseberries or perhaps red currants. If the weather is right, the wines have an acidity that sharpens up their flavor. However, in warm years, such as 1989 and 1990 which were responsible for such marvelous sweet wines further downstream, the wines of Sancerre and Pouilly can lack crispness.

Sancerre and Pouilly do come from opposite sides of the river, so the soil, topography, and microclimates are different. The Pouilly area is on a gently rolling plateau with a chalky clay soil which is generally slightly heavier than that of the sometimes very steep slopes of the Sancerre vineyards. Pouilly-Fumé, which gets its name from the gray, smoke-colored bloom that forms on sauvignon grapes (not from the characteristic smell of gun-flints being struck, as is sometimes reported), therefore tends to have more roundness, weight, and body and can age better than Sancerre.

On the whole, nothing is to be gained by keeping either wine, and both are generally drunk young for maximum freshness (1–2 years old for Sancerre, 2–3 for Pouilly-Fumé), although Pouilly can be good at 4 years and, in exceptional circumstances, can last up to 10. Drink them cool, at about 50–54°F, to bring out their aroma and taste; if they are too cold, their characteristic bouquet and flavor are lost. Excellent aperitifs, they also make fine

DOMAINE VACHERON
Unusually for Sancerre, Domaine Vacheron is better known for its Sancerre Rouge than its white version. For, in a reversal of the normal Sancerrois policy of reserving the best, south-facing slopes for sauvignon vines –

relegating the pinot noir to poor, north-facing plots – the late Jean Vacheron planted pinot noir vines on the choicest, sunniest slopes and lavished much time and effort on making wines with the capacity to age and evolve into deep complex wines of character.
One feature of the vinification which contributes to this, and is only possible because of the amount of concentrated fruit in the wines, is the aging in oak barrels, a proportion of which are new every year. The exact proportion of new barrels and the length of aging time are adjusted according to the style of each vintage.

DE LADOUCETTE
The stylish milestone outside the Château de Nozet explicitly encompasses the profile of Ladoucette wines. The family company owns about 10 times the average Pouilly-Fumé vineyard holding of 15 acres, and sells about 40 percent of the appellation's output under its own label. Large-scale production does not mean low standards: All Ladoucette wines are made to the highest criteria using the best of modern oenological techniques to ensure they are not only of irreproachable quality but also consistent.
In addition to de Ladoucette Pouilly-Fumé, a limited amount (about 100,000 bottles) of a prestige cuvée, Baron de L, is vinified from grapes grown on old vines on choice parcels of land.

(Opposite)
SANCERRE VINEYARDS

accompaniments to goat cheeses (especially local *crottins*) and light summer dishes. The firmer-bodied, more steely wines have a good acidity, making them quite capable of standing up to light, creamy sauces, and some Pouillys work well with chicken.

Only within the last 35 years or so have the wines of Sancerre and Pouilly-sur-Loire become very fashionable. Prices have inevitably risen, and unfortunately the quality has begun to fall, with wines being sold too young and in a "difficult" stage of their maturation. However, a new generation of "serious" wine-makers is now investing time, energy, knowledge, and a great deal of money in making respectable wines.

There is a second, lesser, white from Pouilly-sur-Loire, called Pouilly-sur-Loire and produced from the chasselas grape variety, although each year less and less chasselas are planted as they are more difficult to grow than sauvignon. Neither red nor rosé wines are made there, but before the vineyards were devastated by phylloxera, Sancerre was principally a red-wine producing area. Subsequently, however, it has been found that the soil and climate are better suited to white grape varieties, especially the sauvignon that now accounts for about 80 percent of vineyards planted.

In recent years, *vignerons* have chosen to ignore this experience and have been planting pinot noir to cash in on the vogue for red Sancerre. This is a good example of price not corresponding to quality, for not only are the vines planted in inappropriate sites, but *vignerons* used only to making white wines often do not understand the subtleties of making good red wines. Consequently, the light, charming, fresh fruitiness of which such wines are capable is too frequently marred. Happily there are exceptions (see previous page).

Served cool, a red Sancerre can be a good summer partner for lamb, rabbit, veal, and poultry, as well as light meat *pâtés*. The slightly salmon-pink Sancerre rosé is best served chilled as a thirst quencher.

Southwest of Sancerre there are three small *appellations*, Quincy, Reuilly, and Menetou-Salon, all growing sauvignon grapes and making wines that are very dry, crisp, and characteristically fruity and aromatic, although a trifle more muted than Sancerre (this applies to the price as well!). Each is delicious in its own right, and there are fascinating differences of nuance between them: For example, Quincy wines tend to be lighter. Menetou-Salon is a district on the way up – and worth following – and Reuilly produces some light reds and rosés.

Orléanais wines have to be sought out, for although Orléans once stood among vineyards, rows of more rewarding fruit trees have replaced the vines. The wines that are produced are light and not usually very memorable (the best only reach VDQS status), although some growers are beginning to make surprisingly drinkable wine from chardonnay grapes, called auvergnat blanc locally. However, less than 10 percent of Vin d'Orléanais is white.

The best-known Orléanais wine is made from gris meunier grapes, a red so pale it verges on being a rosé. Drunk when young and lightly chilled, its fresh, slightly earthy taste is pleasant enough for inconsequential quaffing. Other reds are made from the pinot noir and cabernet franc grapes, known locally as auvergnat rouge and moir dur respectively.

GALETTES DE POMMES DE TERRE

Potato Pastries
(Illustrated below)

This recipe is based on the first *galette de pommes de terre* I ever had, the crisp, flaky savoriness of which immediately seduced me. I was to come across quite a few more, many of them severe disappointments, before I learned to reject on sight those that looked dense or greasy – unfortunately all too often the case with mass-produced or carelessly made examples. *Galettes* make excellent snack food, particularly good for picnics: Fill them with

(Below)
Filled galettes de pommes de terre on sale in Romorantin in the Sologne.

cooked onions or mushrooms, sliced tomatoes, ham, or *charcuterie*. Or serve them just as they are, perhaps with a salad.

MAKES 15-18
⅔ cup peeled and diced potatoes
about 1½ cups flour
2½oz chèvre fromage frais or very soft
fresh goat cheese
5 tbsp unsalted butter, softened
1 egg yolk, beaten with 1 tbsp water,
for glazing

Steam the potatoes until tender, then mash them until very smooth. Leave until cold. Mix in just enough of the flour and 1 or 2 tablespoons of cold water, depending on the flouriness of the potatoes, to give a soft, pliable dough.

Blend the cheese with the butter and form into a flat block. On a lightly floured surface, roll out the dough to a rectangle ⅛- to ¼-inch thick. Place the butter-and-

cheese block in the center and fold the long sides of the dough over it. Then fold the bottom third up over the block and the top third down, as like making puff pastry. Seal the edges lightly with a rolling pin and give the dough a quarter turn so the closed seam is to your left, like the spine of a book. Cover and chill. Repeat the entire rolling and folding operation twice more, giving the block a quarter turn each time and letting the dough rest, chilled, between each operation.

Preheat the oven to 375°F.

Roll out the dough to a rectangle just over ¼-inch thick. Using a large sharp knife, cut it into rectangular pieces about 1½-inches wide and 2-inches long, or as liked. Brush them with egg glaze.

Bake for about 20 minutes, until golden. Transfer to a wire rack. When cool, slit them open for a filling, if using, and eat while still warm or cold.

POMMES À LA FORESTIÈRE

Baked Potatoes with Wild Mushrooms

Usually *pommes à la forestière* is a baked dish of wild mushrooms interspersed with layers of sliced potatoes, but for a barbecue in the fall – or indeed for a supper when sitting around the fire at home on a cold night – this recipe for individual baked potatoes is unsurpassed. Serve them very hot and wrapped in clean napkins so no one burns thir hands.

SERVES 4
4 baking potatoes
2 tbsp unsalted butter
½ small onion, finely chopped
thin slice of air-dried ham, chopped

*4-5oz fresh, wild, or cultivated brown mushrooms,
cleaned and chopped
about 3-4 tbsp crème fraîche
freshly ground black pepper
chopped fresh tarragon, chives, or parsley, to serve*

Bake the potatoes in the embers of an open fire, or in the oven preheated to 375°F, for about 1¼ hours or until the flesh is soft and tender.

Meanwhile, melt the butter in a skillet over medium heat. Add the onion and cook 2-3 minutes. Stir in the mushrooms and cook 3-4 minutes longer. Then stir in the ham, crème fraîche, and black pepper and heat through, stirring.

Holding the potatoes in a cloth, cut a slice from the top and, using a teaspoon, press down the flesh to make a small hollow. Divide the mushrooms among the hollows, slowly spooning over the juices so they soak down into the potatoes. Sprinkle with the chopped fresh herbs and eat immediately.

PÂTÉ AU TRAUFFAUDE

Potato Pie

There are many versions of pie, called variously *pâté*, *tourtière*, or *tourton*, containing potatoes. You may come across them locally as *trauffades*, *truffiats*, or *treuffes*. Simpler recipes use stock instead of the crème fraîche or omit either the onion or bacon, or both; more robust, traditional versions make it in a *tourtière* – a type of deep quiche dish much used in Berry. For any version, pâte brisée (which can be bound with milk instead of egg yolks and water; see page 77) can be used instead of puff pastry, and milk can replace the crème fraîche or cream.

*SERVES 4
10oz medium-sized waxy potatoes, peeled
and thinly sliced
9oz puff pastry
5oz sliced bacon, cut across into strips
2 tbsp chopped parsley
1½ tbsp chopped fresh chervil
1 tbsp chopped fresh chives
1 onion, finely chopped
6 tbsp crème fraîche or heavy cream,
warmed gently until very hot*

Preheat the oven to 400°F.

Partly cook the potatoes in boiling salted water for 5 minutes. Drain well.

On a lightly floured surface, roll out just over half of the pastry to an 8-inch round. Trim the edges and place on a dampened baking sheet. Roll out the remaining pastry to make a lid for the pie.

Arrange about one-third of the potato slices on the pastry, leaving the edges clear, and sprinkle with about half of the bacon, herbs, and onion. Repeat the layers, ending with a layer of potatoes. Dampen the edge of the pastry round. Trim the edges from the pie lid and cover the pie. Seal the edges well together, and scallop or flute them. Either cut two large slashes in the top, or cut a large circle of pastry from the center of the lid, but do not remove it.

Bake in the oven about 30 minutes. At the end of this time, ease off the central circle, if formed. Pour the very hot crème fraîche or cream into the pie through the hole left by the circle of pastry, or through the slashes, making sure it flows evenly over and through the potato slices. Replace the circle if removed and return the pie to the oven to bake 10 minutes longer, until the pastry is a rich brown and the potatoes tender. Let stand in a warm place 5-10 minutes before serving.

HARICOTS ROUGES AU VIN ROUGE

Red Beans in Young Red Wine

The young red wine used in this recipe would probably be similar to Beaujolais Nouveau as the same grape variety, gamay, is grown in the vicinity.

*SERVES 4
4 tbsp unsalted butter
1⅔ cups dried red kidney beans or pink beans,
soaked overnight, rinsed, and drained
1 cup young red wine
3oz dried ham, such as Auvergne or Bayonne,
chopped
1 onion, quartered
1 garlic clove, finely chopped
a fresh bouquet garni consisting of 1 sprig of
thyme, 2 small sage leaves, 1 fresh bay leaf, and
several sprigs of parsley
½ cup rillons (see page 76)
1 tsp mignonette pepper
salt
1 tbsp chopped flat-leaf parsley*

Melt half of the butter in a large heavy-based saucepan. Stir in the beans until well coated with butter, then add the wine and 1 cup of water. Bring to a boil and skim off the scum.

Add the ham, onion, garlic, and bouquet garni and boil 10 minutes. Then cover and simmer about 1½ hours until the beans are tender, adding more water if necessary.

Sauté the *rillons* in the remaining butter until hot. Add these to the beans with the mignonette pepper and plenty of salt and cook 15 minutes longer.

Serve the beans with the chopped parsley scattered on the top.

LE GRAND HÔTEL DU LION D'OR**

69 rue Georges Clemenceau
Romorantin-Lanthenay
Tel 54 76 00 28
See recipes opposite and on page 58

M. and Mme Barrat have restored the Lion d'Or building and turned it into an extremely

luxurious hotel; but it is their daughter Marie-Christine and her talented chef-husband Didier Clement, who have created the food for which the restaurant is famed. Marie-Christine studied medieval cooking at university and inspired Didier to experiment with herbs and spices used in those times. Some of these required painstaking research but now many are grown for them locally. Didier incorporates the old-fashioned flavors into his clean, simple style of cooking with innate skill and subtlety.

ÉCHALOTES D'ORLÉANS

Shallots with Vinegar and Honey

(Illustrated on page 50)

SERVES 4
4 tbsp unsalted butter
½lb shallots, preferably gray
¼ cup white wine vinegar, preferably from Orléans
½ cup white wine
1 tbsp honey
salt and freshly ground black pepper
chopped fresh thyme, for garnish

Melt the butter in a heavy-based pan over low heat. Add the shallots and cook gently, shaking the pan occasionally, until translucent and soft.

Stir in the vinegar and boil until it has almost completely evaporated. Stir in the wine and reduce by about two-thirds.

Stir in the honey and seasoning. Check the levels of sweetness and acidity, adding more honey, vinegar, or wine as necessary. Serve sprinkled with thyme.

BROCHET AUX NOISETTES

Pike with Hazelnut Sauce

I first ate this dish when my spirits were not much brighter than the exceptionally dreary late summer weather. The dish looked fresh and bright enough on the plate, but I was still not very enthusiastic when I took the first bite. I immediately exercised my prerogative to change my mind, and devoured it with relish. The rich flavor and texture of the nut-butter sauce was a beautiful companion to the pike in this old Tourangeau recipe.

I have not yet quite been able to recapture that wonderful sauce, for that year's nuts had been unusually good. The ones used in my sauce had been picked after a period of warm sunshine, then spread out on sacking and left in a warm, sunny place for a few days so that the husks came off easily. If you are lucky enough to find a hazelnut tree, you will have some truly fresh nuts with which to effect a proper re-creation.

SERVES 4
1½ sticks unsalted butter, softened, plus more for greasing paper
4 pike fillets
2-3 tbsp dry Vouvray wine
1-2 tbsp lemon juice
salt and freshly ground black pepper
½ cup shelled whole hazelnuts (filberts), lightly toasted, skinned, and very finely chopped
1 egg yolk

Melt 2 tablespoons butter in a large pan. Add the pike, pour in the wine and lemon juice, and season. Cover with buttered parchment paper and poach the fish until just cooked; about 5-7 minutes, depending on the size of the fillets. Remove the fish, cover, and keep warm.

Put the nuts into a mortar and, using the pestle, work in the egg yolk. Gradually stir in the cooking juices to make a smooth sauce. Stir into the pan and gradually beat in the remaining butter.

Alternatively, chop the nuts very finely in a small blender or food processor without letting them become oily. Work in the egg yolk, then slowly pour in the cooking juices. Gradually add the remaining butter to give a smooth sauce.

Season the sauce and add more lemon juice if necessary. Pour the sauce over the fish as it is, or strain it first.

SAUMON DE LOIRE

Loire Salmon with Radish
(Illustrated right)

Because salmon is one of the fish most associated with the Loire, it appears frequently on local menus. However, it does not follow that the salmon served is from the Loire and it certainly will not be if "*de Loire*" is not mentioned, or if it is the fall or winter. At Le Grand Hôtel du Lion d'Or (see opposite), Didier Clement would only use genuine local fish. He teams it perfectly with very thinly cut, peppery-sweet summer radishes, and I have adapted his recipe slightly.

SERVES 1
6 red radishes
5-oz piece of wild salmon, sliced horizontally
into 3 pieces
1 tbsp unsalted butter
juice of ½ lemon
½ cup crème fraîche
salt and freshly ground black pepper

Very thinly slice 4 of the radishes and use to cover the top of each slice of salmon.

Melt the butter in a skillet over medium heat. Add the salmon, radish-covered-side uppermost, and cook about 3-4 minutes, depending on the thickness of the salmon, and its temperature before the start of cooking.

Meanwhile, cut the remaining radishes vertically in half, then very thinly slice these halves. Arrange them on a plate.

Add the lemon juice to the crème fraîche and season to taste.

Reassemble the salmon into one piece, place it in the center of the plate, and spoon crème fraîche over and around it.

COLLIER D'AGNEAU MÈRE GIFFARD

Neck of Lamb with Beans and Mushrooms
(Illustrated far left)

This is the type of "hearty, homey" fare so often associated with the damp, misty image of the Sologne. The characteristic elements that make this welcoming fall or winter dish so memorable are floury potatoes which collapse to make a thick sauce, *haricots demi-secs*, and chanterelles, which each give off their wonderful perfumes and flavors. In the absence of *haricots demi-secs*, use dried white beans and soak them overnight beforehand. If fresh chanterelles are not available, use ½lb chopped cultivated mushrooms with 1oz dried cèpes soaked in hot water 20 minutes, and then drained.

SERVES 4
2 tbsp pork fatback or unsalted butter
1 large onion, chopped
4 carrots, quartered
2 floury potatoes, quartered
1¼ cup dried white beans
9oz fresh chanterelles, well washed
1 sprig of fresh thyme
1 small sprig of fresh wild thyme
1 bay leaf
1 sprig of fresh rosemary
4 lamb shoulder neck slices
salt and freshly ground black pepper
chopped parsley, for garnish

(Opposite, left to right)
Neck of Lamb with Beans and Mushrooms (this page), *with Shallots with Vinegar and Honey* (page 48).

In a large Dutch oven, heat the pork fatback or butter, add the onion, and cook, stirring occasionally, until browned.

Stir in the carrots, potatoes, beans, mushrooms, and herbs. Place the lamb on top, add 2 cups water, and bring slowly to a simmer. Skim the surface, cover, and cook very gently about 1¼-1½ hours, by which time the meat and beans should be tender and the potatoes collapsed to make a thick sauce. Check during the cooking and add more water if necessary.

At the end of the cooking time, check and adjust the seasoning and the amount and consistency of the liquid: if necessary, spoon some off and boil it to reduce it. Serve garnished with parsley.

PÂTÉ DE PERDRIX EN CROÛTE

Partridge Pâté Baked in a Pastry Crust
(Recipe follows overleaf)

Orléans and the lands to the north have long been renowned for their game pâtés en croûte. This is hardly surprising considering the proximity of gently undulating wheatlands, which not only supplied an abundant golden harvest of grain, but also served as a breeding ground for partridges. These are not the gray-legged species native to Britain, but the slightly larger and visually more interesting – though only somewhat gastronomically less appealing – gray-legged "Frenchmen." Unfortunately, modern farming practices often involve removing hedgerows from the landscape and applying chemical pesticides and herbicides, with a consequent decline in the partridge population.

SERVES ABOUT 8
2 partridges, dressed, livers and hearts reserved
3 tbsp marc or brandy
3-4 tbsp chopped mixed fresh herbs
¼lb boneless veal
¼lb lean boneless pork
3oz pork fatback
2 tbsp butter, plus more for greasing mold
2 shallots, chopped
2oz chicken livers
6 tbsp medium-bodied dry white wine
salt and freshly ground black pepper
about 1lb puff pastry
3 eggs, beaten

Remove the meat from the partridges. Cut the breast meat lengthwise into strips, season, pour on half of the marc or brandy, and sprinkle with a pinch of the herbs. Cover and leave in a cool place about 4 hours, turning 2 or 3 times. Grind or very finely chop the remaining partridge meat, with the veal, pork meat and fatback.

Melt the butter in a sauté pan over low heat, add the shallots, cover, and cook gently until very soft but not colored. Add the partridge livers and hearts and the chicken livers to the pan and cook briskly 2 minutes until browned but still pink in the center. Stir in the remaining marc or brandy and set it alight. Using a slotted spoon, transfer the shallots, livers, and hearts to a plate and let cool.

Stir the wine into the cooking juices. Boil a couple of minutes and then cool. Grind the liver mixture, and add to the other ground meats with the wine and seasoning. Leave overnight.

The next day, preheat the oven to 375°F.

Roll out three-quarters of the pastry and use to line a buttered hinged pâté mold about 9 x 5 inches in size, pressing it well into the angles and leaving 1 inch overhanging all around. Roll out the remaining pastry for a lid.

Add the remaining herbs and 2 of the eggs to the ground meats. Press half the mixture over the bottom of the mold, then arrange the partridge breast strips down the center. Cover the breast meat strips with the remaining ground mixture, piling it in a dome.

Fold the overhanging pastry over the filling and put the pastry lid in place. Seal the edges well and brush with the remaining beaten egg. Make a small hole in the top and insert a foil "chimney" to allow steam to escape.

Bake 20 minutes, then reduce the temperature to 350°F and bake 45 minutes to 1 hour longer. Cover with foil or a double thickness of parchment paper if the pastry begins to brown too much.

Let cool before unmolding. Keep in a cool place for a day before serving.

CHEVREUIL AU SANCERRE ROUGE

Venison in Red Sancerre

The most popular way of serving venison I have come across in all manner of restaurants in the region, from simple *fermes auberges* to high-class establishments, is the classic *grand veneur*. Done well, it can indeed be a splendid dish "fit for a king." However, it is a very lengthy process, so I am giving a simpler recipe, one that you are more likely to cook but which is sure to be enjoyed with just as much relish.

I like to cook venison, as well as other game, in a red Sancerre because it produces a lighter dish than those in which more traditional heavier wines are used. I use the same recipe for smaller cuts.

SERVES 8-10
1 haunch of venison, weighing about 7-8lb
3-oz piece of salt pork or unsmoked slab bacon, cut across into strips
3 shallots, chopped
2 young carrots, chopped
1 celery stalk, chopped
a fresh bouquet garni consisting of 1 bay leaf, 2 sprigs of thyme, 2 parsley sprigs, and 1 sprig of rosemary
salt and freshly ground black pepper
1 bottle of red Sancerre wine
4 tbsp rendered pork fat or unsalted butter
1 cup game stock

Using a sharp knife, make slits in the venison at intervals and insert the strips of pork or bacon. Place the haunch in a deep bowl. Add the vegetables and bouquet garni. Season and pour in half of the wine. Cover and leave in a cool place 24 hours, turning the meat from time to time.

Preheat the oven to 400°F.

Remove the venison from the bowl and pat dry. Strain the marinade and reserve both the wine and vegetables.

In a roasting pan, heat the pork fat or butter and add the vegetables. Brown them over high heat, stirring frequently. Using a slotted spoon, remove them and reserve. Add the venison to the pan and brown it all over. Lift it out, put the vegetables and herbs in the pan, and then lower the venison back again. Baste it with some more wine.

Roast in the oven about 15 minutes, then lower the temperature to 350°F and continue roasting a total of 9 minutes per pound, including the initial period at the higher temperature. Baste frequently with the remaining wine. Transfer the venison to a warmed plate, cover, and keep warm. Stir the remaining wine into the cooking juices and boil until syrupy. Stir in the

(Left)
The recipe for Pheasant with Cèpes below is excellent for older birds, but a young tender one can be roasted. Here at the Hôtel St-Hubert on the road to Cheverny, a young bird is nearly ready to be served with a sauce made from the cooking juices, stock, and some local wine.

Remove the pheasant from the dish and pat dry. Reserve the marinade but discard the herbs from it.

Heat the remaining oil in a large skillet with a lid or a Dutch oven into which the pheasant pieces will fit snugly. Cook the bacon and remaining onion in it over fairly low heat, stirring occasionally, until the onion has softened. Using a slotted spoon, transfer to a paper towel. Evenly brown the pheasant 2 pieces at a time. Transfer to paper towels. Cook the mushrooms in the pot, stirring occasionally, then transfer to paper towels. Pour off excess fat from the pot.

Stir the remaining vinegar into the cooking liquid and boil until well reduced, then stir in the reserved marinade. Allow to bubble a few minutes. Add the stock, bring to a boil, and skim.

Lower the heat. Put half of the bacon mixture, half of the mushrooms, and 1 reserved thyme sprig in the bottom of the pot. Place the pheasant on top, then add the remaining bacon mixture, thyme sprig, and mushrooms. Cover tightly and cook over a very low heat, or in the oven preheated to 325°F, for about 1½ hours.

Transfer the pheasant and mushrooms to a warmed dish. Boil the cooking juices until well reduced, adding any juices from the pheasant which collect on the serving plate. Over low heat, gradually stir or whisk in the butter. Season to taste and pour or strain over the pheasant.

stock and reduce, until lightly syrupy. Add any juices that have collected on the plate around the venison.

Strain the sauce into a warmed gravy boat and serve with the venison.

FAISAN AUX CÈPES

Pheasant with Cèpes

Containing the spoils of much-loved hunting, this dish brings together two of the most popular autumn foods, both of them eagerly sought wherever there is suitable terrain almost the whole length of the Loire. It is an ideal way of cooking older birds, or those of indeterminate age, to make a casserole good enough for the finest dinner party. Partridges are equally delicious cooked in this way.

SERVES 3-4
1 pheasant, dressed and cut into pieces
3 tbsp oil
¼ cup red vinaigre d' Orléans
1 bay leaf
3 sprigs of fresh thyme
a small sprig of fresh rosemary
1 large onion, chopped
1¼ cups red Sancerre wine
salt and freshly ground black pepper
4 slices of bacon, chopped
½lb fresh cèpes, trimmed and cleaned
1½ cups chicken stock
2 tbsp unsalted butter, diced

Fit the pheasant pieces into a non-metallic dish. Pour on half of the oil and half of the vinegar. Scatter the herbs, reserving 2 of the thyme sprigs, and half of the onion on top. Pour in the wine and season lightly. Cover and leave in a cool place 8 hours.

CANARD SAUVAGE AUX COINGS

Wild Duck with Quince

(Illustrated left)

This recipe is based on an evocative account of a dish described to me by an old French friend during wistful reminiscences of the wonderfully scented dishes his wife used to prepare when they were first married. She also made *eau-de-vie de coing* and he suspected that some of that was added to the marinade. Fragrant quinces are the key to success.

SERVES 4-6
1 large or 2 small-to-medium-sized ripe quince(s)
2 mallards, green glands removed
1¼ cups medium-bodied dry white wine, such as a
Chenin Blanc
salt and freshly ground black pepper
6 tbsp unsalted butter
2 shallots, finely chopped
⅔ cups chicken stock
pinch of sugar
squeeze of lemon juice

Wipe the down from the surface of the fruit, then peel, core, and slice it, reserving the trimmings.

Put the ducks into a Dutch oven and tuck the quince slices around them. Pour in the wine, cover, and leave in a cool place 8-12 hours, turning the birds occasionally.

Preheat the oven to 350°F.

Simmer the quince trimmings in 1¼ cups of water for 15 minutes. Strain the juice and set aside. Lift the birds and quince slices from the pot. Pour off and reserve the wine. Season the ducks.

In the Dutch oven, melt 2 tablespoons of the butter. Add one-third to three-quarters of the quince slices with the shallots and sauté them about 3-4 minutes. Remove. Add another 1 tablespoon butter to the pot, then add the birds, breast-side down, and brown them lightly. Turn them over carefully and lightly brown the undersides, too.

In a saucepan, bring the wine, strained quince juice, and stock to a boil. Pour this over the duck, cover the pot tightly, and cook in the oven about 45 minutes until the ducks are tender, turning them over halfway through.

In a skillet, melt another 2 tablespoons of butter, add the remaining quince slices, and fry about 10 minutes until golden and tender, turning them over halfway through to cook them all over.

Transfer the ducks to a warmed plate. Purée the contents of the pot and reheat gently. Swirl in the remaining butter. Taste and adjust the seasoning, adding a little sugar or a squeeze of lemon juice if necessary to lift the flavor.

Serve the duck with the purée and the slices of quince.

LAPIN DE GARENNE À LA SOLOGNOTE

Stuffed Wild Rabbit

SERVES 4
1 wild rabbit, dressed and skinned, with the liver,
kidneys, and heart retained
a handful of mixed fresh herbs, including parsley,
chives, and chervil, chopped
1¼ cups Loire Sauvignon wine
5 tbsp unsalted butter
2oz lightly smoked bacon, chopped
1 small shallot, finely chopped
¼lb mushrooms, preferably fresh wild ones or
cultivated brown mushrooms, chopped
⅔ cup chopped cooked Swiss chard or
spinach leaves
salt and freshly ground black pepper
2 small carrots, chopped
2 onions, quartered
½ cup veal stock
a bouquet garni

Put the rabbit in a bowl and scatter some of the herbs over it. Pour in the wine, cover, and leave in a cool place overnight.

Remove the rabbit from the marinade and pat it dry, reserving the marinade. In a saucepan, melt 1 tablespoon of the butter, add the bacon, and cook over fairly low heat until the fat runs. Finely chop the rabbit liver, kidneys, and heart, and add these to the pan with the shallot and mushrooms. Increase the heat and cook 3-4 minutes, stirring. Stir in the Swiss chard or spinach, along with the remaining chopped herbs and seasoning.

Place the rabbit on its back. Spoon in the stuffing and fold the meat of the sides over the stuffing. Sew up the opening with thick thread or fine string and truss with the legs neatly tucked in.

Heat three-quarters of the remaining butter in a Dutch oven into which the rabbit will fit comfortably. Add the rabbit and brown it lightly. Lift it out. Add the carrots and onions to the pot and brown these lightly, then place the rabbit on top. Pour in the stock and add the bouquet garni. Cover and cook gently about 1 hour, until the rabbit is tender.

Transfer the rabbit to a warmed plate and keep warm. Stir the reserved marinade into the cooking juices and boil until slightly syrupy. Lower the heat and gradually swirl in the remaining butter. Adjust the seasoning. Remove the stuffing and serve with the rabbit cut into pieces, and the sauce strained over the top.

(Top)
In Orléanais, apple-growing is not especially
intensive, but there are plenty around for such
classics as tarte Tatin.

TARTE DES DEMOISELLES TATIN

Upside-Down Apple Tart
(Illustrated left)

To make a true country-style tarte Tatin, the apples should be cut into large chunks, not paper-thin slices. The sisters (see page 37) cooked their tarte in a metal "oven" placed over charcoal and this produced the characteristic caramelization of the sweetened buttery apple. Modern ovens will not produce the same effect so, nowadays, the apples, butter, and sugar are usually browned over direct heat before being covered with pastry and baked. Our tart was photographed at the Hôtel St-Hubert. If using a baking pan, and especially if using gas, make sure the apples don't stick and burn.

SERVES 6-8
1½ sticks unsalted butter, diced
1 cup + 2 tbsp sugar
6 firm tart-sweet apples, peeled, cored, and
halved or quartered
squeeze of lemon juice, optional
¾lb puff pastry or pâte sucrée (see page 90),
chilled

Using about 4 tablespoons of the butter, thickly butter the bottom and sides of a 9-inch tin-lined copper tarte Tatin mold about 2-inches deep, or a heavy skillet or sauté pan that can go into the oven, or a thick-bottomed baking pan. (The buttering is easiest if the butter is diced.) Sprinkle with ¾ cup of the sugar.

Arrange the apples in the mold or pan and sprinkle with the remaining sugar and butter. Cook over high heat for 15 minutes until the apples are tender and the butter and sugar thickened and golden brown. Remove from the heat, add the lemon juice and let cool, removing some liquid if there is too much.

On a lightly floured surface, roll out the pastry to a round about ½ inch larger in diameter than your mold. Prick it with a fork, place it on a baking sheet, cover, and chill 30 minutes.

Preheat the oven to 425°F. Cover the apples with the pastry, tucking it down the sides of the mold or pan.

If using puff pastry, bake 12-15 minutes, then lower the temperature to 350°F and bake for 10-12 minutes longer until the pastry is risen and crisp. If using pâte sucrée, bake 25 minutes.

Let cool a few minutes, then invert onto a warm plate and serve warm.

GÂTEAU DE PITHIVIERS

Almond-Filled Pastry Cake

(Illustrated on page 32)

SERVES 6-8
1lb puff pastry, thawed if frozen
1 egg yolk beaten with 1 tsp cold water, to glaze
confectioners' sugar, for sprinkling
FOR THE FILLING
1 cup ground almonds
6 tbsp granulated sugar
3oz unsalted butter, softened
2 egg yolks, beaten
2 tbsp dark rum

Make the filling: Work the almonds with the sugar in a food processor to make a paste. Spoon this into a bowl and beat in the butter followed by the egg yolks and rum. Cover and chill very well.

Divide the pastry into two portions, one slightly larger than the other. On a lightly floured surface, roll out the smaller portion to a round about 10 inches in diameter. Trim the edges and very carefully transfer to a baking sheet.

Roll out the other piece of pastry to a similar round and trim the edges. Place the almond filling on the first round, leaving a border of about 1 inch clear all the way around. Brush the border with beaten egg. Place the second round of pastry centrally over the filling and press the pastry edges together to seal well. Make a scallop effect around the edge and a slit in the center.

With the point of a sharp knife, starting at the center and working to the edge, score the surface of the pastry in curved, half-moon-shaped lines to give the traditional appearance – but be careful not to cut right through. Brush the top with the egg glaze, avoiding the scored lines. Cover and chill 30 minutes.

Preheat the oven to 425°F.

Bake the pie about 20 minutes, then lower the oven temperature to 400°F and bake until the pastry is risen and golden brown, 15 minutes or so longer.

Preheat the broiler. Sprinkle confectioners' sugar over the surface of the pastry and broil about 3 inches from the heat until the sugar has caramelized, 1-2 minutes. Carefully, transfer to a wire rack.

PAIN D'ÉPICES

Honey Spice Cake

(Illustrated on page 41)

Although it is not traditional, I like to eat pain d'épices spread with butter or cream cheese.

MAKES 1 CAKE
butter, for greasing
1⅔ cups flour
½ cup rye flour (or use all white flour)
2 tsp baking powder
1 tbsp ground cinnamon
½ tsp ground ginger
pinch of salt
2 eggs, beaten
⅔ cup honey, warmed until liquid
1 tsp finely crushed aniseed

Preheat the oven to 375°F and butter a 9- x 5-inch loaf pan.

Sift the flours, baking powder, spices except the aniseed, and salt into a bowl. Form a well in the center and pour in the eggs and honey. Add the aniseed and gradually draw the dry ingredients into the liquid to make a smooth batter. Pour into the prepared pan and bake in the oven until a skewer or thin knife inserted into the center comes out clean, about 40 minutes.

Remove from the oven, let cool about 5 minutes, and then turn out onto a rack.

FINANCIERS DE SULLY

Almond Cakes from Sully

Another version of this recipe coats the top of the cakes with frosting after cooling, but I find this additional sweetness spoils the chewy-nuttiness of financiers, rather than adding anything to them.

MAKES ABOUT 20
2 egg yolks
6 tbsp granulated sugar
3 tbsp flour
⅓ cup ground almonds
4 tbsp unsalted butter, melted and cooled, plus more for greasing
½ cup sliced almonds
confectioners' sugar, for sprinkling

Preheat the oven to 350°F.

In a large bowl, beat the egg yolks with the granulated sugar until very thick and mousse-like.

Sift the flour over the surface, then, using a large metal spoon, gently fold it in with the ground almonds and butter.

Butter a 9 x 6-inch baking pan and sprinkle half the sliced almonds over the bottom. Evenly cover with the almond batter and sprinkle the remaining almonds over the surface.

Bake in the oven about 30 minutes.

Cut into fingers and let cool slightly before turning onto a wire rack. When cool, sprinkle with confectioners' sugar.

(*Above*)
*With such a long history of an abundant
variety of fruits, putting it by is in
the blood and many a pantry will have a
row of tempting bottles.*

PANNEQUETS DE FRAMBOISES

Raspberry Crêpes

(*Illustrated far right, with the restaurant's own
pâté des fruits*)

This is one of the most popular desserts
served at Le Grand Hôtel du Lion d'Or
(see page 48). Both the crêpes and the
sauce may be made well in advance.

SERVES 4
1 cup flour
pinch of salt

3 eggs, beaten, plus 3 egg yolks
2 cups milk
7 tbsp granulated sugar, to taste
about 5 tbsp unsalted butter, melted
1½ pints raspberries
½ cup crème fraîche
2 tbsp confectioners' sugar

Put all but 1½ tablespoons of the flour
into a bowl, stir in the salt, and make a
well. Add the whole eggs and stir in 1 cup
of the milk to make a smooth batter.

Whisk together the egg yolks and granulated sugar. Blend a little of the remaining milk with the reserved flour, then
whisk into the egg yolk mixture. Scald the
remaining milk, then slowly stir into the
egg yolks. Return to the rinsed pan and
heat, stirring, until thickened, then cook
gently for about 2 minutes, still stirring.
Strain the custard into a bowl and let cool,
stirring occasionally.

Press the raspberries through a non-
metallic strainer to make a purée.

Stir 3 tablespoons of the melted butter
into the batter. Heat the remaining butter
in a crêpe pan or small skillet, coat the
pan, and then pour the excess into a bowl
to use again. Add a small ladleful of batter,
swirl it around, then cook quickly until
lightly colored on the underside. Turn
the crêpe over and cook the other side.
Remove and keep warm while making a
total of 16 crêpes.

Just before serving, preheat the broiler.
Stir the crème fraîche into the custard,
and flavor with a little raspberry purée.
Place a spoonful of this in the center of
each crêpe and fold into four.

Sprinkle the folded crêpes with confectioners' sugar and place them under
the hot broiler until the sugar melts to a
glaze. Pour the remaining purée over 4
plates and arrange 4 crêpes on each.

"THE ENCHANTED LAND"

THROUGH TOURAINE, THE HEARTLANDS OF THE VAL-DE-LOIRE

TOURAINE IS A LAND OF SIMPLE ELEGANCE AND QUALITY. WARM BALMY DAYS AND EVENINGS AND WIDE BLUE HORIZONS GRACE A CALM COUNTRYSIDE OF meadows, fields, and woods, dotted with châteaux and producing lush harvests of fruit and vegetables, fine goat cheese, and gentle wines.

The majority of the fruit, early vegetables, and vines are planted on the rich, fertile, and well-drained soil near the Loire, and along the valleys of its tributaries. To the south, there are rolling hills with yellow fields of giant sunflowers and corn. These hills open out after Loches to the plateau of Ste-Maure, with its quiet pastoral appeal. In summer, herds of sleek brown goats, looking like small deer, graze on the usually lush pastures to provide the rich milk for the region's many *fromages de chèvre*. There is also a wealth of good poultry and game, and more cattle than nearer the Loire.

(Opposite) The famous kitchen garden at Villandry features only produce available in the sixteenth century. Box hedges mark out the nine vegetable patches.
(Above) Plates or baskets displaying a variety of brightly colored, sparkling pâtes des fruits are a frequent sight in pâtisseries all along the Loire. Made from local, sun-ripened fruit boiled down with sugar, they are quite delicious.

The Tourangeaux are polite, charmingly friendly, and hospitable. They also quietly pride themselves on speaking the purest French. As Touraine has the highest concentration of popular châteaux along the Loire, tourists flock there and tourism is a major source of revenue. However, most stay in and around the châteaux towns, and if you move slightly away you will find tranquil beauty and unspoiled villages.

From the air, the land looks like a piece of lace. Weaving across its surface there are many small streams flowing into rivers which, in their turn, flow into the Loire. This network has its influence on the food, keeping the pastures well watered and providing bountiful catches for fishermen.

Along the Creuse, a tributary of the Vienne, local farmworkers moor their punts so they can supplement their income by spare-time fishing. As the river bed has ideal lurking places for big fish, there are pike and pike-perch. In summer, however, the particular prize is gray mullet which comes all the .way up from the Atlantic. A local fisherman told me that whereas shad stay in the Loire, the mullet prefers to fork right into the Vienne.

At La Chapelle, one of the tiny old river ports with a terraced stone *levée* sloping down to a quay, I spotted a few cabined punts. Investigation showed these to be owned by local fishermen who still earn a reasonable amount netting salmon in spring and catching eels, bleak, and pike at other times. In Chaumont, I was introduced to the handful of locals, both young and old, who net or line-fish commercially from small punts. Their catch includes gudgeon,

1 Decorative ironwork from a hotel window. 2 An early morning drink in a bar during the Sunday morning market in Langeais. 3 Apples piled up in the market in Tours. 4 Cakes on display in Maison Poirault, rue Nationale, Tours, where you can watch handmade sweets being made. 5 An architectural feature on the town hall building, Tours. 6 Tobacco plants are grown in sunny spots along the Loire and the Cher. The harvested leaves are hung in special sheds to dry, then supplied to the French National Tobacco Company. 7 Mural at Le Coq Hardi, Monnaie, north of Tours. 8 Artichokes on sale at Tours market. The vegetable was a favorite food with François I's court at Amboise; at a wedding feast in 1575, his daughter-in-law, Catherine de' Medici, ate them until she almost burst. 9 A selection of goat cheeses on sale at Tours market, and including the famous log-shaped Ste-Maure. Not only are there many different goat cheese producers, but also many different styles.

1	2		3
	4	5	6
7	8	9	

bleak, and roach for *Friture* (see page 114) in the spring, or large fish caught under licence from the bigger flat-bottomed boats called *toués*. These have cabins at the stern where fishermen used to live for weeks at a time.

In the gentle waters of the Indre gliding past Azay-le-Rideau, a few carp still lead the same leisurely existence as they did when Catherine de' Medici's chefs created *Carpe à la Chambord* (see page 81). Although carp caught in rivers do not get as fat as they do living an even more sedentary life in ponds, their flesh can have a fresher flavor.

Rarely mentioned in the same breath as salmon, shad, and carp when talking of fish in the Loire area, perch are, however, prized in Touraine. Although handsome, the spines on the first dorsal fin can be quite unpleasant and the scales stubborn if not promptly removed. However their taste, especially that of smaller fish, is well worth the trouble, and it is certainly worth choosing them on the rare occasions that perch appears on restaurant menus.

The family pig has not yet vanished from the countryside, although it is now not necessary for a family to raise and fatten its own pig during the spring and summer to provide the household with food during the lean winter months. Those homes with a smallholding or large backyard often still cosset and pamper their own pig until it is in prime condition for the ceremonial killing and ritual transformation into all manner of good things: some fresh for eating immediately, such as *boudins noirs*; some for keeping a few days; others to last longer, packed in fat or cured with salt. These occasions were family affairs. Everyone would know his or her role, whether it was separating the rind from the fat, cutting up strips of fatback, filleting, grinding, or immersing meat in the salt bath. An enormous *fait-tout* slowly bubbled and steamed on the stove while the family got on with the business of making pâtés, *boudins*, *rillettes*, and their crisp cousin *rillons* (or *rillauds* or *rillots*, as they are called in some places).

Rillettes are a cross between pâté, potted meat, and a purée (see pages 66 and 76). They are made throughout the region, and in Anjou. Although many places, such as Tours, claim to be their "home," or to make the *vrai* or best, the truth is probably that there is no one birthplace, and no one place where they are invariably better than elsewhere. They have been made since at least the fifteenth century, when the kitchens of large houses would have a circular depression formed in the brick floor for the fire, with an inner rim to support the huge *rillettes* cauldron. Cut out of one side was a step, so that the pot could be reached more comfortably during the long, laborious job of stirring a large batch.

The pork for *rillons*, described by Balzac as "residue of pork fried in its own fat,

(Above)
BAR CHARLES VIII
The bar entrance at the Hosten et Restaurant Langeais.

(Opposite)
FISHING ON THE RIVER
You may see this type of boat moored against a line of nets across the river. A long spar, a balancier, is pivoted over the bow and a carrelet, a net resembling a square, upside-down umbrella, hangs from it, submerged. The fish swim along the nets to find a way through, only to pass over the carrelet, making it vibrate and so alert the fisherman. Experience allows him to differentiate between flotsam, small fish, or big fish. If the latter, he quickly trips the balance so that the carrelet, with its fish, is whisked from the water.

RILLETTES

The meat used in rillettes is usually pork, but it can also be duck, goose, rabbit, or game, or a mixture of any of these with pork. The proportions of fat to lean can vary from half to almost equal parts, and flavorings can range from just salt to a small pinch of quatre-épices, a bouquet garni, or some chopped onion – which I was told by Gilbert, a portly prize-winning charcutier, is vital for the mixture's acidity.

Nearly every maker will have his own recipe, and make his own choice of what quality and cuts of meat to use. The appearance of the rillettes is a fairly good guide to quality: Be very wary of factory-made examples, because the process and equipment used reduce the whole thing to an unpleasant homogeneous mass. Rillettes are generally eaten with foods with contrasting textures or "bite," such as fresh crusty bread, a crisp salad, and pickled walnuts or cornichons.

resembling cooked truffles," is cut into large cubes and sometimes may be salted and left a few hours to pickle slightly before cooking. Often the bones are left in the meat to add flavor. The cubes are baked very slowly until the meat is just tender – not soft – so most of the fat is expelled and they become crisp and crunchy (see page 76). The *rillons* are then packed into sterilized pots, the reserved fat poured around them, and left to set. *Rillons* are eaten hot with fried apple rings or a tangy applesauce and puréed potatoes, or cold with a crisp salad, piquant mustard, and a glass of chilled dry Vouvray.

If pigs' blood is available, *boudins noirs* will be made, but in Touraine *boudins blancs* are more often seen. Sitting in a *charcuterie*, usually on a white tray, *boudins blancs* look most uninspiring, and their appearance does not do justice to what has been dubbed the "queen of sausages." They are made from white meat, such as chicken or veal, enriched with pork fatback and crème fraîche and bound with eggs and bread crumbs (an exception among French sausages). The traditional seasoning is delicate white pepper, perhaps with a little onion and some *quatre-épices*. Added champagne, brandy, or *foie gras* are affectations happily not rife in the Loire. Here, herbs are sometimes added to the *boudin* mixture, or the *boudins* rolled in them after initial cooking. *Boudins* may be eaten right away, because they are poached by the *charcutier*, but it is more normal to reheat them by grilling or frying.

Andouillettes are about the same size as *boudins blancs* and are also bought ready-cooked. Their base is pigs' innards, to which a wide variety of flavorings is added. Although basically made of the same ingredients as *andouilles*, they contain more fat and are larger. They are usually brined and sometimes smoked, and sold in slices for eating cold.

In the south, the small town of Richelieu, named after the seventeenth-century cardinal and statesman, also acquired a reputation for the quality of its *charcuterie*, in particular its potentially confusingly termed *jambon de volaille*. This was not chicken cured in the manner of ham, but chicken legs boned, stuffed, and cooked in white wine.

Richelieu's royal master, Louis XIII, used to stay at the Château d'Amboise, northeast of Richelieu's own town, because of the proximity of the hunting in the popular Forêt d'Amboise. While at the château, for some unknown reason, he had a penchant for cooking for himself – there is no evidence to suggest that he did this elsewhere. Either he only ever fancied something plain to eat or he had an extremely limited repertoire of dishes, because he usually made a simple onion omelet moistened with a little local red wine.

Charles VIII, an earlier occupant of the Château d'Amboise, played a much more pivotal role in the gastronomic history of the Loire, because he was responsible for the introduction of several products to the region. Among the many things which captivated him when he was in Italy, attempting to annex Lombardy, were their food and their gardens. In 1495, after one of his forays, he included many specimens of fruits, vegetables, seeds, and plants in his convoy of treasures, scholars, and experts. Among the latter was one who knew about breeding chicken in incubators, a practice then unknown in France. Not surprisingly, the vast train of 6,000 mules was ambushed and looted at Fornova.

Fortunately, many plants, such as artichokes, survived and later took to the favorable climate and well-watered fertile soil of their new home at Amboise. They grew well and quickly became popular, spreading throughout the whole region and into Anjou. The chicken expert also survived the ambush and his now-ubiquitous system was put into practice at Amboise in 1496.

With plenty of rich aristocrats in the great houses and châteaux, coupled with the presence of Tours and good transportation links to the lucrative markets of Paris, the industrious inhabitants of Touraine quickly saw the potential for growing rare vegetables and fruits. Nowadays we make a fuss about *primeurs* vegetables, but as long ago as the sixteenth century, there were market gardeners, known locally as *bêcheux*, who specialized in them. As well as artichokes, superb, thick white-stemmed asparagus is a particular specialty, with the region coming second only to the Gard in volume produced.

Celery is also a major commercial crop, although of little gastronomic significance. However, some of the rows of barren banks of earth which look as if they might be hiding celery heads may instead be concealing a crop of cardoons (see page 80), because these are grown like celery – the stems buried in banks of earth to keep them white and give them their delicate texture and delicious flavor. When harvested, cardoons look like prickly celery that has had an overdose of fertilizer. They belong, instead, to the thistle family and taste vaguely like their close relation the artichoke. The outer stems and leaves of cardoons are removed before use, leaving the inner, more tender ones, and the hearts. The latter are sometimes referred to locally as *moelle végétale* and are served cut into rounds as a garnish. Confusingly, the classic recipe *cardons à la moelle* combines cardoons with a rich, red-wine

(Below left)
THE FAMILY PIG
Even though Touraine is known for a number of pork products, such as rillettes and rillons, and pork dishes, such as porc au pruneaux, and even though the need for a home supply of food throughout the winter no longer exists, an individual "family" pig kept on a smallholding, or even in a backyard, is a far more likely sight than a large pig farm.

(Below right)
DRYING THE WASHING
Dish towels hanging on a line in a backyard near Villaines-les-Rochers.

(Top)
PLUM TART

(Above)
WILD MUSHROOMS
*Many different types of wild
mushrooms grow, each one in its
own specific habitat.*

(Right)
PEARS AND WALNUTS
*Winter varieties of pears and fresh
walnuts are often used together in
cooking, particularly in fruit tarts,
because they taste very good in
partnership. These were
photographed in the grounds of the
château at Azay-le-Rideau.*

sauce containing beef marrow (*moelle*). This magnificent, silvery-white vegetable is, sadly, less popular today than it used to be – partly due to the poor monetary yield in relation to the space required to grow it.

Certain varieties of beans, such as *michelets*, are allowed to grow until they mature into full-sized white beans, ready for eating toward the end of summer. They are picked and sold in their shells. The fiddly job of shelling them is still considered worth the trouble, since they are creamier and more delicate than dried white beans, and can be cooked without pre-soaking.

Some full-sized white beans would have been preserved for the winter in a large stoneware pot, called a *potte* or *tinette*. The beans were peeled and washed, then layered alternately with salt in the pot and covered with water and white vinegar, a plate placed on top to keep the beans submerged. The *potte* would then have been left in the cellar, or similar very cool place, to be dipped into when fresh vegetables were scarce. One of the few fresh regional winter vegetables was the black radish, which had the additional advantage of storing well up to four months.

At one time, the larger, coarser peas of the region were treated in the same way as beans, because they were more suited to eating dried than fresh. In the middle of the seventeenth century, however, the small tender green pea developed by Italian gardeners during the Renaissance was introduced, possibly by Catherine de' Medici's Italian chefs. The new variety was named *petits pois* in France to distinguish it from its fat cousins.

Italy was also the source of some of the virtual catalogue of fruits of which Touraine proudly boasts. For instance, Bon Chrétien pears arrived in the late fifteenth century at the Château de Plessis-les-Tours. The pear was introduced by Saint François de Paul. At the age of 70, he had been persuaded by the extremely ill Louis XI to leave Cantabria, in Italy, as the king believed the saint's prayers would improve his health. He was wrong, and he died in the saint's arms in 1483. However, the goodness of the saint's life was such that he was known as *"le bon chrétien"* (the good Christian), and the pear of which he was so fond was named after him.

In Blois, at the beginning of the sixteenth century, the greengage, or *reine-claude*, was also introduced from Italy and developed by Pierre Belon. It was originally known as the *"prune de la reine Claude"* (the plum of Queen Claude), because the first in France were served at the feast celebrating the wedding of locally born Claude, at the age of 15, to the future François I, and named in her honor. Later, in 1515, she became Queen of France and took the sweetly perfumed, yellow-green, rose-flushed fruits to her heart. Not only did she have many trees planted herself, but she also encouraged others to grow them in warm, sheltered, sunny spots, and often even supplied the young saplings. There are other varieties of gages, such as the reine-claude de Bavay, bred by one of Napoleon Bonaparte's retired generals, which ripens later.

Ordinary plums arrived in the Loire much earlier than gages. Crusaders

CHOCOLAT POULAIN

The original chocolate factory was opened in Blois in 1848 by Auguste Poulain, in the days when its raw materials were brought up-river from Nantes. Poulain made a valiant attempt to

revive the shipping of the Loire as late as 1898. Only two battered chalands were still using the port, one selling pottery from Gien, the other bringing apples from Anjou. Poulain commissioned a special flat-bottomed, narrow-draft, 130-foot steam tug built at Nantes. For 10 years "Fram" regularly chugged up and down to Nantes, bringing cocoa and sugar for the factory: seven tons in her own hold, seventy in the barge she towed.

No one else followed Poulain's example, and the company eventually had to revert to cheaper rail transport.

brought them back from Damascus, hence damascenes and damsons. The climate and soil were just right, and the trees flourished. Surplus fruit was dried and stored for winter use. The St-Catherine-de-Fierbois, also known as "*petit Damas*," was particularly popular for this purpose. By the sixteenth century, prunes from Touraine were much in demand in Paris, especially at Lent, and they were even mentioned by Rabelais.

However, growing plums and preparing prunes is not the most assured and profitable way of earning a living in an area where there is an easier livelihood to be gained from growing apples and pears. Long gone are the days when every country housewife gathered the plums from her own trees before sunrise, so they were still covered with dew, and then spread them on wicker trays to leave them in the sun to dry. The drying was completed by putting them each day in the dying heat of the old-style heavy ovens until they were "*demi-fraidi*," turning them from a plump, rich purple to shiny, wrinkled, and black. Small, golden, rose-flushed, juicy, and tasty mirabelles were, and still are to a lesser extent, popular around Blois. They were at one time dried for sweetmeats called "*pistoles*."

Melons were introduced into France somewhat earlier – by the Romans. The reputation of melons grown in the "garden of France" began to take hold during the reign of Henry IV. This was perhaps due to the reputed practice of feeding the melons with honey-water! Langeais melons gained a reputation for themselves in Paris and elsewhere and they were given the nickname of "*sucrins*," derived from *sucre*. An entry in John Evelyn's diary, made during the summer of 1644, when he was staying in Tours, reads, "We have now a store of those admirable melons, so much celebrated in France for the best in the kingdom." Melons played such an important role within the community that three were incorporated into the town's coat-of-arms. Today, melons are grown on south-facing hillsides near Langeais, and you can buy them – still warm, succulent, and sweet – from many roadside stalls or from local markets.

The traditional pastries of Touraine, *cordes* (small braided disks), *russeroles* (fritters), *cassemuses* or *casse museaux* (muzzle breakers) – so called because of their hardness – and *fouaces*, date from the Middle Ages, and the last two were mentioned by Rabelais. In one of his tales, he tells of a confrontation between some *fouaciers* who were taking their wares to market in Parilly, near Chinon, just before the *vendange*, and some shepherds guarding the grapes against the depredations of birds. The shepherds tried to buy some of the *fouaces*, but the *fouaciers* refused, very rudely, so a fight ensued. This won the shepherds their *fouaces*, but resulted in a war.

Originally, *fouaces* were baked in the ashes in the hearth (*focus*, hence the name). Nowadays, they are baked in ovens, and basic recipes vary from characteristically Rabelaisian

(Above)
TUREENS, VOUVRAY
Chef-patron Bernard Copin of the Auberge du Grand Vatel, is President de la Touraine Gourmande, a group of restaurateurs whose aim it is to provide good-quality local food.

(Opposite)
CHÂTEAU DE CHENONCEAU
When Catherine de' Medici took possession after the death of her husband, Henri II, her chefs introduced their own Italian ways and ingredients.

(Top and above)
GOAT CHEESES
Ste-Maure (top) is the best-known cheese of the region, helped in some large measure, since 1974, by the efforts of members of the Commanderie de Ste-Maure de Touraine.

ingredients of butter, egg yolks, saffron, and spices, to simple, plain flat yeast cakes which are best eaten hot with butter or a rich soft cheese and, perhaps, some good home-made fruit confiture. Fouaces can be more interestingly flavored with orange-flower water, and I have also seen quite a number of "fancy" yeast breads based on fouace dough.

In the heyday of the Loire river trade, because of the availability of the basic raw materials, several chocolatiers – including France's largest chocolate company, Poulain, whose advertising billboards with their distinctive horse emblem will be familiar to anyone who has visited France – set up in business in Blois. To this day, the town is famous for its chocolate and chocolate confections, and it still boasts several good chocolatiers and pâtissiers. Chocolate-lovers are particularly advised to take a stroll along the rue Denis-Papin. This street was named after a Blésois doctor and engineer who, realizing the potential of steam, created the pressure cooker. His "marmite de Papin" was originally intended as a means of extracting nourishment from bones by cooking them at temperatures above boiling point, but its full range of uses in cooking food developed later.

A local chemist, Jean-Antoine Chaptal, Comte de Chanteloup and one of Napoleon Bonaparte's ministers, developed the process of adding sugar to wine in order to strengthen it, and so immortalized his own name in the term "chaptalization." He also invented the process for extracting an inferior type of sugar from sugar beet when Napoleon's blockade of the West Indies resulted in shortages.

CHEESES

Driving through the region, especially in the south, the roadsides are dotted with signs announcing the sale of farm-made goat cheese, leaving you in no doubt that Touraine is goat cheese country. The cheeses can vary quite substantially, as can the farms. Some are very hygienic and organized; some milk by hand, others by machine; some keep the goats "free-range," others house them under semi-intensive conditions in barns. Goat cheese has been made here since at least the ninth century, when Charlemagne commented upon it, and later Rabelais recommended local "talmouze aux fromages de bique" while Balzac mentions the cheese of Ste-Maure. This town is still the center of production, processing some 25,000 barrels of goats' milk a year. Since the turn of the century, Friday has been the day local farm cheese-makers sell their products in its old market place. There is now also a cheese festival there during the first weekend in June.

Originally Ste-Maure cheese was made only on the Ste-Maure plateau in and around the town. Later it was also produced in Anjou, Charente, and Poitou, with a resultant debasing of the quality and name. Since July, 1990, however, it has been protected by an *appellation d'origine contrôlée* limiting its area of production. Produced both on farms and in factories, Ste-Maure is a log-shaped cheese, about 6 inches long and 1½ inches in diameter, with a typical, very white paste. The characteristic straw running lengthwise through each cheese was intended to prevent it from breaking up. Made from lightly salted fresh whole milk, it may be eaten fresh, after just 10 days, when it is soft and moist. It is *"demi-affiné"* after about three weeks maturing, or once it has developed a white downy surface; it then has a light texture and pleasantly mild flavor which is not at all goaty.

Ste-Maures with grayish rinds are more mature cheeses, about two months old, and have a stronger, more distinctly goaty flavor. The logs may also be rolled in wood ash for Ste-Maure *cendré*.

Selles-sur-Cher is also protected by an AOC, but the area of permitted production extends beyond the small town after which it is named. Even so, it is quite strictly limited. The cheese is made in a disk, about 4 inches across and 1¼ inches high, and has a soft, light texture and an attractive mild, fresh flavor. The *cendré* version is aged longer and is a little smaller as a result (water is lost during storage). It has a firmer texture and a more pronounced taste. Valençay is a different shape again – a low, truncated pyramid – and it has a richer texture and stronger flavor than Selles-sur-Cher.

Pouligny-St-Pierre is another farm-made *appellation contrôlée* cheese, pyramid-shaped. When young, the cheese has a clean, slightly salty taste, with a hint of straw, but the flavor can become quite distinctive as the cheese matures.

There are many more cheeses in various shapes – logs, cones, disks, and drums – usually quite small, fresh, and light textured. They are produced in small quantities, as and when there is milk or when it is convenient to do so. Many farms make no attempt to sell their cheeses beyond displaying a roadside sign, so almost every time you buy goat cheese or try some in a restaurant, you will have a completely new selection to choose from and wonderful new flavors to savor.

WINES

There are about 20–25,000 acres of vines in Touraine, with wines from only about one-third to half of this area entitled to the simple *appellation* "Touraine." They are generally light, fruity wines, for serving chilled and quaffing on a warm summer's day. More red than white is made, although the latter is generally better. Most important, and usually most enjoyable, are the white sauvignon wines. Flowery, fresh, and at its best distinctly aromatic, Touraine Sauvignon can make a reasonable alternative to Sancerre and Pouilly-Fumé, at a

PAUL BUISSE

Through four generations and for nearly 90 years, the fathers and sons of the Buisse family have been *négociants* in Touraine. The highly regarded company is concerned about quality, restricting their portfolio to the Loire and specializing in AOC wines.

Young wines are bought from selected independent *vignerons* and stored in tufa cellars. For the core *Cuvées Prestiges* range, hundreds of samples of wines are rigorously analyzed and tasted by six professionals. The prides of the range, for which Paul Buisse has been responsible, are his *Cristal*, a very fine Sauvignon, and Chinon and Bourgueil *vieilli sous bois* (matured in old oak casks). These two demonstrate the aging potential of good red Touraine wines.

CHÂTEAU DE
MONCONTOUR

*To produce clean, fresh-tasting,
young white wines, cool, even
temperatures and stainless steel
vats (stainless steel is inert) are
both necessary. At Château de
Moncontour, very large vats have
recently been installed in the tufa
caves, where the right conditions
exist naturally.*

more affordable price. The red equivalent is Gamay de Touraine. Made from the same grape as Beaujolais, good examples can be equally fruity, but more sensibly priced. Chilled, they make good summer quaffing wines or accompaniments to casual summer foods and light meat or poultry dishes.

There is also a Touraine *appellation* for sparkling wine, both white and rosé, but many producers prefer to follow the stricter specifications required for Crémant de Loire, and so reap a greater profit.

The sites for the higher *appellation* red and white wines are divided by Tours, with red wines to the west and white wines to the east. Vouvray, the most famous white Touraine wine, comes from vineyards on the north bank of the Loire, and these produce some truly delicious wines – unfortunately, there are also some not very good ones.

The vines grow on limestone and tufa plateaux, which form such thick strata in places that not only are there wine cellars hewn out of the cliffs, but also three- and four-storey dwellings. In 1644, the diarist John Evelyn observed with amusement that he had seen plumes of smoke billowing from chimneys among the vines.

All Vouvray wines are made from chenin blanc grapes, so have the characteristic fruity, flowery flavor underlined with an acidity that prevents them being cloying and gives them the ability to last and mature beautifully for many decades. However, Vouvray is made in every style, still and sparkling, from dry through several shades of sweetness to, in exceptional years, luscious sweet dessert (*moelleux*) wines. The degree of ripeness determines the potential style, but which style is made also depends on the wine-maker. *Moelleux* wines are labor intensive, thus costly, and, despite their high quality, have only a limited market. So only *vignerons* with an established reputation find them a commercial proposition.

Vouvray is served cool rather than heavily chilled, and the degree of sweetness usually governs the age at which it is drunk. Dry Vouvray can be drunk young, as an aperitif or first-course wine; medium-dry Vouvray about three to four years after the vintage, is ideal as an accompaniment to rich fish, such as salmon, and lightly creamy dishes. Sweet Vouvray, on the other hand, improves with keeping, maturing to a golden hue and developing the rich scent of quince and cooked plums that makes it delicious with fruit desserts, or sipped on its own. Sparkling Vouvray is made by the *méthode champenoise*, as is the slightly effervescent *pétillant*. Montlouis, on the opposite river bank, produces similar but lighter wines.

The best-known red wines of Touraine – indeed of the Loire – are produced west of Tours from the vineyards of Bourgueil, St-Nicolas-de-Bourgueil, and Chinon. They are made principally from cabernet franc grapes, but up to 2 percent cabernet sauvignon is permitted. These three areas produce light, fruity red wines, in which some people claim to be able to detect nuances of raspberries, currants, wild strawberries, and violets (although these attributes are only discernible in mature, well-made wines of good vintages).

Bourgueil wines have a tendency toward austerity, which makes them a little difficult to enjoy when young. Although sometimes drunk a year or two after the vintage, they are usually better if left five years or more to allow them to soften to a more delicate fruitiness. St-Nicolas-de-Bourgueil wines are usually somewhat lighter, especially when young, although the subtle bouquet can develop with age.

There are two styles of Chinon, and both have greater finesse than either of the Bourgueils. On the hillside, the porous tufa subsoil produces firm, full-bodied wine which benefits from three to four years aging and can last up to 10; while the mixture of sand and gravel on the plain yields lighter wines ready for drinking sooner. With their balance of tannin and fruit, I find Chinon red wines particularly good for cooking. Beef and game dishes, for example, are lighter made with them than with Burgundy or Bordeaux-style wines. Bourgueil, St-Nicolas-de-Bourgueil, and Chinon also all produce dry rosés, and from Chinon there is also a rare white wine.

(*Below and below left*)
GASTON HUET
I have been drinking Gaston Huet's wines longer than any other Loire wines, as I knew early on that they could be superlative.
Now, with the assistance of his son-in-law Noel Pinguet, M. Huet makes all styles of Vouvray. Although all are excellent, he is particularly lauded for his sweet wines, especially the ambrosial *moelleux* wines made only in great years. Vouvray and Touraine wines generally owe Gaston Huet (the "t" is pronounced) a big vote of thanks, as he has traveled

tirelessly promoting them at the same time as his own wines. Moreover, the other wines must have benefited from the high caliber of his products. Now nearer 90 than 80, he has relinquished the post of Mayor of Vouvray he held for many years and does not jet across the Atlantic so often, but still lives life more fully and happily than many younger men.

SALADE DE RILLONS

(Illustrated above)

A mention of *rillons* never fails to have one of two effects on me — either sending me into a reverie as my mind flies to memories of Tourangeau days, or making me voluble, as I recount to anyone at hand the innumerable joys of the region.

As La Cave Martin (see opposite) is right in the heart of Touraine, it is not surprising that they know that the best way to serve rillons is on a bed of salad, accompanied by a crisp, dry Touraine Sauvignon.

SERVES 4
2oz pork fatback or good-quality lard, diced
2lb fresh side pork, cut into chunks
6 allspice berries
1 bay leaf
1 sprig of fresh thyme
¼ cup light olive oil
salt and freshly ground black pepper
1½ tbsp white wine vinegar
1 tsp chopped fresh herbs
1 tsp Dijon-style mustard
a generous selection of well-flavored salad leaves, to serve

Preheat the oven to 300°F.

Melt the fatback or lard in a baking dish large enough to hold the pork in a single layer. Add the pork and turn the pieces to coat them with fat. Tuck in the allspice, bay leaf, and thyme, and season. Pour in water to a depth of ¼ inch, cover the dish with foil, and bake for about 3 hours, basting occasionally, until the pork is very tender.

Drain off the liquid (this can be strained and the fat separated from the water for use in cooking). Increase the oven temperature to 425°F and return the pork to the oven to bake until lightly browned. Remove it from the oven.

Make a dressing by whisking together the oil, vinegar, herbs, and mustard and season well. Arrange the salad leaves on a large serving plate, place the *rillons* on top, and trickle the dressing over the top.

RILLETTES

(Illustrated on page 66)

Rillettes are very easy to make at home. If sealed tightly with fat, they can be kept in the refrigerator for serving as a snack, as a first course, or for a light lunch. Crisp, dry Loire Sauvignon wines or dry Vouvrays are ideal accompaniments as they counterbalance the fattiness of the *rillettes* and add a contrasting fruitiness. The *rillettes* I make do not have as high a fat content as many found in France.

SERVES 6
¼lb pork fatback, chopped
2¼lb boneless pork butt, plus some bones
1 shallot, chopped
1 sprig of fresh thyme
1 bay leaf

pinch of quatre-épices
salt and freshly ground black pepper

Preheat the oven to 275°F. Put the fatback into a heavy casserole and heat it in the oven until melted.

Cut the pork into small pieces and add to the fat with the bones, shallot, herbs, spices, seasoning and ⅓ cup of water. Cook very slowly (the fat must not bubble) in the oven about 4 hours, stirring occasionally, until the meat is almost falling apart. Add more water if it appears to be getting too dry.

Remove the bones and herbs. Drain the meat in a strainer and reserve the fat. Using a fork, tear the meat into fine shreds. Pack these into sterilized stoneware pots, leaving a little room for a sealing layer of fat.

Remove the reserved fat which will have settled from the juices. Heat and pour over the *rillettes* to seal out the air.

Store in a cool place, but bring to room temperature to serve.

TARTE TOURANGELLE

Rillettes Quiche

The idea of a quiche containing *rillettes* was not one that immediately appealed to me because it seemed to have all the ingredients for a fatty but fairly flavorless mouthful. I avoided examples that looked as if they would live up to my expectations. However, when I saw Daniel Poirer's *tarte Tourangelle* in the covered market in Tours, I snapped up a portion and was very glad that I did, because it was well flavored, light, and not at all greasy. The secret, of course, lies in the quality of the *rillettes*.

SERVES 4-6
FOR THE PÂTE BRISÉE
1¼ cups flour
pinch of salt
1 stick unsalted butter, softened and chopped
2 egg yolks
FOR THE FILLING
2 extra large eggs, beaten
6 tbsp crème fraîche
7 tbsp milk
1½ tbsp chopped parsley
2 tsp chopped fresh chives
salt and freshly ground black pepper
¾ cup rillettes, *see left*

Sift the flour and salt onto a work surface and make a well in the center. Put in the butter and egg yolks and quickly blend them together with your fingertips until the mixture looks like rough scrambled eggs. Draw in the flour, chopping it through with a round-bladed knife, then mix to a smooth dough. Shape into a ball. Wrap and chill about 30 minutes.

On a lightly floured surface, roll out the dough and use it to line an 8-inch quiche pan. Prick the bottom and chill 30 minutes longer.

Preheat the oven to 375°F with a baking sheet inside it. Place the quiche pan on the baking sheet and bake 15 minutes.

Remove the pastry case from the oven. Lower the oven temperature to 350°F. Let the pastry cool.

Beat together the eggs, crème fraîche, milk, herbs, and seasoning.

Roughly dot the *rillettes* over the bottom of the pastry case and spread them out. Place the quiche pan on the hot baking sheet again. Pour in the egg mixture, and bake for 25-30 minutes until just set in the center.

Serve warm or at room temperature, but not chilled.

LA CAVE MARTIN
La Vallée Coquette
Vouvray
Tel 47 52 62 18
See recipe far left

La Cave Martin is tucked away on the hillside behind Vouvray, but signs from the N152 on the way to Tours show the way up the winding country lanes. Although Edith and Philippe Bellanger had no restaurant experience before they bought the *ferme auberge* in the early

1980s (they both worked in offices), their accomplished cooking of regional dishes, such as *andouillettes au Vouvray* and *rillons*, have made them firm favorites with local *vignerons*. The couple have an unusual working partnership – he cooks the main courses, while she does the first courses and desserts. Of note for the summer is a good-sized terrace outside.

BOUDINS BLANCS, POMMES EN L'AIR

White Sausages with Apple Slices
(Illustrated far right)

Boudins blancs are the classic white sausages found all over the Loire region. The recipe that follows serves them on a bed of glistening, golden apple slices that have been literally tossed "in the air" – to prevent them from absorbing too much butter while they are fried. This is traditionally served as a first course, but it also makes an excellent light lunch dish.

MAKES ABOUT 14 4-inch SAUSAGES
2oz crustless pain de campagne or similar white bread (not pre-sliced, steam-baked bread), torn into pieces (about 2 cups)
½ cup crème fraîche
1 shallot or ½ small onion, finely chopped
½lb skinless, boneless chicken breast
6oz pork fatback
½lb lean boneless veal or pork, such as fillet end of leg
2 egg whites, lightly beaten
1 tbsp chopped parsley
leaves from 2 sprigs of fresh thyme, chopped
leaves from 2 sprigs of fresh marjoram, chopped
1½ tsp chopped fresh chives
pinch of quatre-épices or ground mace
salt and freshly ground black pepper
about 3½ yards of sausage casings
milk, for poaching (optional)
unsalted butter, for frying
3 small, tart-sweet apples, peeled, cored and sliced

Soak the bread in the crème fraîche until thoroughly moistened, then beat until smooth. Grind the meats and fat together. Mix in the shallot or onion, the bread mixture, the egg whites, herbs, spices, and seasoning. Leave in a cool place about 3-4 hours, then chill well.

Fill the sausage casings with the meat mixture, taking care not to over-fill them. Twist and tie at intervals of about 4 inches. Knot the ends.

To cook the sausages, bring to a boil a large saucepan of water or a mixture of 2 parts water to one part milk. Lower the heat so that the water is just simmering, add the boudins, and poach gently about 10-12 minutes. Prick carefully with the point of a needle as they rise to the surface. Drain well and cool quickly.

Next day, separate them into individual sausages. Brush with melted butter and broil, turning frequently, until heated through; or fry in butter until light golden brown all over. Transfer to a warmed plate, cover, and keep warm.

If you have fried the sausages you can use the same pan to fry the apples, although you may need to add more butter; if you have broiled them, melt some butter in a skillet. When hot, add the apple slices and cook quite briskly until light golden brown on one side. Turn them over and cook the other side. Transfer the apples to a serving plate. Either place the sausages on top of the apples, or serve them separately.

(Right)
White Sausages served with Apple Slices (this page), and Brioches au Fromage Frais de Chèvre (page 91). In a region where there seem to be more goats than cows, fresh goat cheese may replace the butter usually used in the making of brioche. With a slight savoriness and light delicate crumb, the result is quite delicious.

FÈVES À LA TOURANGELLE

Fava Beans with Ham

(Illustrated on page 87)

Some versions of this dish use a glass of white Touraine wine instead of the bean cooking water, but if you are using the fresh young beans for which this recipe is intended, I think the wine detracts from the flavor of the vegetables.

Serve this dish as an accompaniment to plainly cooked meats or poultry, as a first course, or for a light supper dish with good buttered bread.

SERVES 4
½lb shelled young fava beans
5 tbsp unsalted butter
5-oz piece of slab bacon, diced
24 small onions
2 egg yolks, beaten
1 chopped mixed tbsp fresh summer savory,
chervil and parsley
salt and freshly ground black pepper

Blanch the beans in boiling salted water 5 minutes. Drain, reserving the liquid.

Meanwhile, melt the butter in a large heavy-based saucepan pan over low heat. Add the bacon and onions and cook gently, shaking the pan occasionally, about 10 minutes without allowing the onions to color. Add the beans and enough of their cooking liquid almost to cover, reserving the rest, and simmer gently until the vegetables are just tender and most of the liquid evaporated.

Blend 2 tablespoons of reserved bean liquid into the egg yolks. Over low heat, stir this mixture into the beans. Cook gently, stirring, until lightly thickened. Stir in the herbs and adjust the seasoning, then serve at once.

CARDONS TOURANGEAUX AU GRATIN

Cardoons with Mushrooms

After initial boiling to make them tender, cardoons are usually finished in some other way, such as simply sautéing them in butter 10-15 minutes, perhaps with a final sprinkling of herbs, or dressing them with a béchamel sauce. They may also be cooked, as here, layered with mushrooms – a vegetable with which they have an affinity. I always serve this as a simple light meal, but it can also be a vegetable accompaniment to fish or meat.

SERVES 4-5
2¼lb cardoons
juice of 1 lemon
5oz large mushrooms, preferably brown or butter,
finely chopped
salt and freshly ground black pepper
3-4 tbsp dry bread crumbs
1 stick unsalted butter

Discard the coarse outer leaves and "strings" from the cardoons. Separate the outer stems from the heart. Cut the stems into 2- to 3-inch lengths.

Cook the pieces of cardoon in lightly salted water, acidulated with some of the lemon juice about 25 minutes. Drain, and refresh under cold running water.

Preheat the oven to 350°F.

Chop some of the outer stems finely and mix with the chopped mushrooms and seasoning. Layer this mixture with the remaining cardoons in a buttered baking dish. Cover with bread crumbs.

Melt the butter with a little lemon juice, pour this all over the bread crumbs, and put into the oven for about 25 minutes until lightly browned and crisp.

CÔTES DE BLETTE AU GRATIN

Swiss Chard Ribs with Eggs and Cheese

Swiss chard, or côtes de blettes, or blettes, is popular locally. An old Tourangeau name is poirée à carde, which refers to the preferred rib section of the leaf, without its green ruff. Here, tangy chèvre cheese transforms it into a rich first course, or an accompaniment for plainly cooked meats.

SERVES 4
2lb Swiss chard
2 egg yolks
1¼ cups crème fraîche
3 tbsp unsalted butter
3oz soft goat cheese, chopped
salt and freshly ground black pepper

Strip the green leaves from the chard ribs and keep for another dish (see page 55, or use them in place of spinach). Remove the strings and the white covering skin from the ribs. Slice the ribs into 1½-to-2-inch pieces.

Blend the egg yolks with 1 tablespoon of crème fraîche.

Melt the butter in a heavy-based saucepan, add the chard ribs, cover, and cook gently 15 minutes. Add the remaining crème fraîche and cook 10 minutes longer, uncovered. Add the cheese and heat gently until it has just melted into the crème fraîche.

Preheat the broiler. Remove the pan from the heat and immediately stir in the egg yolk mixture gently. Season, using little salt but plenty of black pepper. Transfer to a gratin dish and broil until lightly browned.

CARPE À LA CHAMBORD

Carp with Red Wine

Carpe à la Chambord is a dish of the classic French culinary repertoire. It was devised by Catherine de' Medici's Italian chefs in the kitchens at the Château de Chambord to moisten the compact flesh of the locally abundant carp, and to introduce flavor, for carp, although it can be insipid, does absorb other flavors well.

The dish involves stuffing a carp with veal or whiting forcemeat, larding the fish with bacon, and braising it in red wine with herbs and a *mirepoix*. A sauce is then made from the cooking liquid to serve with the fish. However, if you see *carpe à la Chambord* on a menu nowadays it is unlikely to be the classic dish. It will probably be a portion of carp simply served with a red wine sauce, *beurre rouge* (*beurre blanc* made with red wine instead of white), or perhaps braised in red wine. If a stuffing is included, it will probably be the same type of mixture as that used in *quenelles*, a light fish and cream mousse. *Saumon à la Chambord* usually means portions of salmon, such as steaks, served with a red wine sauce; the fish may also, perhaps, have been cooked in red wine.

This version of *carpe à la Chambord* is a successful compromise for modern tastes and practicalities.

SERVES 4
1 carp, weighing about 3½lb, dressed,
3-oz piece of slab bacon, cut across into strips
salt and freshly ground black pepper
1 stick + 2 tbsp unsalted butter, diced
¾ cup mixed diced vegetables, including carrots, shallots, and leeks
2 cups Gamay de Touraine wine
a bouquet garni

Using the point of a sharp knife, make small incisions in the flesh of the fish. Insert a piece of bacon into each cut. Sprinkle the fish with freshly ground black pepper.

In a heavy-based saucepan or Dutch oven large enough to hold the fish, melt 2 tablespoons of the butter. Add the vegetables and cook gently for about 4 minutes until softened.

Stir in the wine, bring to a boil, and then adjust the heat so the liquid is barely simmering. Add the carp, bouquet garni, and more black pepper and cook the carp gently about 25 minutes, or until the flesh near the bone just flakes when tested with the point of a sharp knife. Carefully transfer the fish to a warmed plate and keep warm. Bring the liquid to a boil, skim the surface, and then boil until reduced by about one-third.

Strain, then reheat but do not boil, and gradually whisk in the remaining butter. Taste and adjust the seasoning, and serve with the carp.

(Left)
Usually rainfall is adequate to ensure that fruit and vegetables thrive, but in drought years artificial watering may be needed. Successive dry summers can leave the Loire itself dismally low.

(Above)
Serious fishing is still a reality and can bring in a pleasurable income, because Loire fish are highly prized in the region and much in demand.
Top restaurants willing to pay top prices to be able to add the captivating words "du Loire" after the fish on their menus.

FILETS DE PERCHE À LA PURÉE D'ORTIES

Perch Fillets with Nettle Purée

Having a late picnic breakfast one clear spring morning, I absent-mindedly watched a fisherman casting into the Cher, but didn't take much notice. After making one catch, he pulled on a glove, wandered to some clumps of young nettles in the hedges near the river bank, and very carefully selected small leaves from the tops of young shoots. Obviously they were not for feeding to an animal. He returned to his fishing.

Intrigued, I ambled up and wheedled my way into idle conversation. The nettles were to make a sauce to accompany the perch he had just caught. His grandmother always prepared a similar sauce in the spring because she maintained that nettles were a good springtime tonic, being rich in vitamins and minerals. He liked to wait until perch came back into season, because he thought the salty, tangy flavor of the nettles made such a good combination with the flavor of the fish.

When tiny flowers start to appear on the nettles, the flavor changes and they no longer make good eating.

SERVES 4
3 tbsp unsalted butter
2 small shallots, finely chopped
1 cup finely chopped tender, young nettle leaves
¼ cup medium-bodied dry white wine
¼ cup fish stock
⅔ cup crème fraîche
salt and freshly ground black pepper
1¾lb perch fillets, skinned and any small bones carefully removed

Melt half of the butter in a heavy-based saucepan over a low heat, add the shallots, and cook gently, stirring occasionally, until softened.

Add the nettles and continue to cook gently 1 minute, stirring occasionally.

Stir in the wine and stock and boil until reduced by half. Add the crème fraîche and reduce until lightly thickened.

Purée, then strain if liked and season. Reheat gently.

Melt the remaining butter in a skillet over medium heat, add the perch and cook 1 minute on each side.

Season, place on warmed plates, and pour the sauce over and serve at once.

COURGETTES FLEURS FARCIES

Stuffed Zucchini Flowers

(Illustrated opposite)

Tours is a very busy university city, with a fast link to Paris (1 hour 40 minutes by TGV), yet it is possible to bask in clear warm sunshine on the terrace of Jean Bardet's restaurant (see page 84), eating vegetables grown within a few yards and packed with bright flavors. To devise this recipe for pike-perch, he needed to look no further than his own garden for home-grown zucchini plants, vegetables, and beautiful sun-ripened tomatoes. In my city garden, the air is so smog-filtered that my tomatoes and herbs never develop much flavor.

SERVES 6

about 1-1¼ lb wild pike-perch or salmon fillet, cut into 18 pieces
salt and freshly ground black pepper
18 zucchini flowers, stamens removed
7 tbsp unsalted butter
1 cup finely chopped carrots
½ cup finely chopped onions
1 cup finely chopped white part of leek
1 cup finely chopped celery
¾ cup white wine or fish stock
12 slim zucchini, halved
peeled tomatoes, for garnish

Season the fish and place a piece carefully inside each zucchini flower.

Melt 2 tablespoons of the butter in a sauté pan, add all the vegetables except the zucchini, and cook, stirring occasionally, until softened but not colored.

Add the wine or stock and boil until reduced by half. Press through a fine strainer. Return to the clean pan. Heat to just below a simmer. Carefully add the zucchini flowers and cook gently about 3 minutes. Transfer to warmed plates.

Meanwhile, blanch the zucchini in boiling salted water. Drain, refresh under cold running water, drain well again, and thinly slice lengthwise, cutting almost through to the end. Melt 3 tablespoons of the butter in a skillet, add the zucchini and heat through. Fan out on the plates with the flowers. Swirl the remaining butter into the juices in the sauté pan, then pour this sauce over the plates.

Garnish with peeled tomatoes.

JEAN BARDET **
57 rue Groison, Tours
Tel 47 41 41 11
See recipes on page 82-3
and right

Jean Bardet, with his engaging
and unpretentious enthusiasm,

so obviously appreciates the
good things in life. Although he
comes from Charente, he loves
living and working in Touraine,
because of the wide range of
excellent local produce and
wines available.
Since 1989, he has turned his
attention to the garden that
surrounds his hotel and
restaurant in the middle of
Tours. He and his three
gardeners have successfully
grown over 60 different herbs
and many varieties of vegetables
and fruits. Eels and carp are
stocked in one of the ponds and
wildfowl swim on another. He
also keeps a pig and some
plump chickens and geese. He
serves his *amuse-bouches* (above)
on spoons as an *hors d'œuvre*.

BROCHET RÔTI AU FOUR, AU VIN DE NOIX

Roast Pike with Walnuts

(Illustrated left)

Jean Bardet of the eponymous restaurant in Tours (see far left) cooks the potatoes for this dish in goose fat, giving them a particularly rich flavor which complements the leanness of the pike; failing that use duck or good pork fatback. He also uses *eau-de-noix des Pères Chartreux*, a deliciously versatile drink well worth adding to the shopping list when in France. A similar homemade liqueur can be prepared by steeping 12 freshly peeled walnuts in 1 pint of brandy for 2 months. At the end of this time, add ¾ cup sugar, and leave for a further month, then strain and re-bottle.

SERVES 4

3oz goose fat, duck fat, or pork fatback
1¼lb potatoes, sliced, rinsed, and dried
1 onion, finely chopped
2 small fresh bay leaves, cut into strips
salt and freshly ground black pepper
4 tbsp unsalted butter
4 pike fillets
1½ cups fish stock
about 3 tbsp eau-de-noix
⅓ cup chopped walnuts
lemon juice
fresh thyne and bay leaves, for garnish

Preheat the oven to 350°F. Heat 2 ounces of the fat in a flameproof baking dish, and add the potatoes, onion, and bay leaves. Season, place a piece of butter in the center, and brown in the oven.

Heat the remaining fat in a skillet over medium heat, add the pike, and cook about 2 minutes on each side until lightly golden. Season, place on the potatoes, and cook in the oven a further 10 minutes.

Meanwhile, melt 2 tablespoons butter in a heavy-based saucepan, add the nuts, and cook 1-2 minutes. Pour in the stock and boil until reduced by about half. Add *eau-de-noix* to taste and boil briefly to obtain a light sauce. Over low heat, swirl in the remaining butter. Season and add lemon juice to "lift" the flavor.

Transfer the potatoes and fish to 4 warmed plates, then pour the sauce over the top. Garnish with fresh herbs.

MATELOTE

Fish in Wine

Matelotes are found all along the Loire, and date from the days when it was an important commercial route. They were originally served to the Loire boatmen (*matelot* means sailor or mariner) when they tied up in the small ports or at the many riverside hotels and restaurants.

A *matelote* is not a soup. It is more like a stew in that the liquid should be concentrated and full of flavor; but the fish should be lightly cooked, not "stewed."

Matelotes are most often associated with eels, but they can contain almost any freshwater fish; they may even contain veal, as in *Matelote des Tonneliers* (page 118). The wine will be that produced locally, so it may be red or white, crisp, or full and fruity, with each type changing the character of the *matelote*. Additional ingredients may simply be onions and mushrooms; there may also be bacon, and sometimes prunes are added in, usually if eel is the fish (if the wine is red, this variation is sometimes called *bouilleture*).

SERVES 4

3lb mixed freshwater fish such as young eel, carp,
tench, perch, and trout, dressed
6 tbsp unsalted butter
1 onion, sliced
1 carrot, sliced
2 cups dry Vouvray wine
a fresh bouquet garni consisting of 2 sprigs each of
parsley and thyme, a sprig of tarragon, and 1
bay leaf
salt and freshly ground black pepper
about 3oz button mushrooms
chopped fresh chervil or parsley, for garnish

Fillet the fish and cut them into 1½-inch pieces, reserving the bones, skin, and heads. Melt 4 tablespoons of the butter in a wide, shallow pan. Add the onion and carrot and cook over fairly low heat, stirring occasionally, until softened.

Stir in the fish bones, skin and heads to coat them with butter, then add the wine, bouquet garni, seasoning, and 1¼ cups water. Bring to a boil, skim, and then simmer until reduced and well flavored (no more than 20 minutes at the most!). Remove the fish heads, skin and bones.

Adjust the heat so bubbles are just breaking on the surface of the liquid, then add the fish in the order given, allowing the liquid to return to its original temperature before adding the next fish. Cook gently about 8-10 minutes, until the flesh just flakes easily.

Meanwhile, melt the remaining butter in another pan, add the mushrooms, and cook, tossing occasionally, 4 minutes.

Discard the bouquet garni from the *matelote*. Serve in warmed wide bowls, with the mushrooms and chervil or parsley scattered over the top.

If liked, the *matelote* can be finished by swirling in some extra diced butter, or crème fraîche, just before serving.

PÊCHES TOURANGELLES À LA ROYALE

Poached Peaches with Raspberry Sauce

(Illustrated right)

Sun-ripened peaches and sweet raspberries from Touraine's fertile soil and long summer days give the true regional flavor to this dish. Recipes specifying raspberry jam or red currant jelly, instead of fresh berries, are "interlopers" from elsewhere or appropriate to other seasons.

SERVES 4
4 ripe peaches
about 1¼ cups vanilla-flavored sugar
strip of lemon peel
1½-2 pints fresh raspberries
¼ cup crème fraîche

Pour boiling water over the peaches and leave about 10-20 seconds. Lift the fruit from the water and peel off the skins. Cut the fruit in half and remove the pits.

Put the peach halves in a saucepan and add just enough water to cover them. Add ½ cup sugar for every 2½ cups of water, and the lemon peel. Bring to a simmer and poach the peach halves in this syrup 5 minutes until tender. Using a slotted spoon, remove the peaches and let them cool. Then place them in a dish, cover, and chill.

Press the raspberries through a non-metallic strainer, reserving a few whole ones for garnish. Whip the crème fraîche until it stands in soft peaks, then add vanilla sugar to taste. Stir in the raspberry purée. Add more sugar, if necessary. Serve the peaches with the sauce poured on top. Garnish with the reserved raspberries.

MACARONS DE CORMERY

Macaroons

(Illustrated right)

Macaroons are, of course, made in many places, but those of Cormery, or, more specifically, the abbey there, are legendary. A hot ember that jumped from the fire and burned a hole in the cook-monk's habit, exposing his navel, was read by the abbot as a sign from Saint Paul to help him distinguish the abbey's macaroons from those of local bakers who were cashing in on their popularity. From then on, the abbey's macaroons were distinguished by a swirl in the center.

MAKES 20-25
¾ cup almonds, blanched and ground
¾ cup vanilla-flavored superfine caster sugar
½ teaspoon rice flour or cornstarch
2 egg whites
sheets of rice paper

Preheat the oven to 375°F.

Mix the almonds, sugar, and rice flour or cornstarch in a bowl. Add the egg whites and, using a wooden spoon, mix all the ingredients together. Leave a few minutes, then beat again briefly.

Lay sheets of rice paper, rough side down, on baking sheets. Using a teaspoon, place small mounds of the almond mixture on the rice paper, allowing plenty of room between them. Mark a small swirl in the top of each mound.

Bake in the oven 15-20 minutes, until light and dry on the outside but still slightly sticky in the center.

Carefully remove each macaroon from the rice paper. Let to cool on a wire rack. Serve with cool crème fraîche or *fromage blanc* and fresh juicy strawberries.

TARTE AUX POIRES

Pear Tart

(Illustrated right)

There are innumerable versions of pear tart: large, small, round, rectangular; some with sliced fruit, others using halved pears; some with a cushion of custard beneath the pears, others with the fruit sitting directly on the pastry. They may even be embedded in a luscious almond mixture, as here. To make a tart that is more easily divided into smaller portions, slice the pears after poaching and before sprinkling with the alcohol, and then arrange the slices in even, concentric rows on the pastry.

SERVES 8-10

FOR THE PÂTE SUCRÉE
1½ cups flour
¼ cup vanilla-flavored confectioners' sugar
7 tbsp unsalted butter, softened and chopped
2 egg yolks

FOR THE FILLING
1 egg white, beaten
1¼ cups vanilla-flavored granulated sugar
2 ripe-but-firm Bartlett or Comice pears
3 tbsp eau-de-vie de poire Williams
(pear Brandy)
1 stick + 2 tbsp unsalted butter, softened
4 egg yolks
¾ cup blanched almonds, ground
2½ tbsp flour

Sift the flour and sugar onto a work surface and make a well in the center. Put in the butter and egg yolks and quickly blend them together using your fingertips, until the mixture looks something like rough scrambled egg. Draw in the flour, chopping it through with a round-bladed knife. Knead lightly until smooth, then form into a ball. Cover and chill for at least 30 minutes.

On a lightly floured surface, roll out the pastry dough and use to line a 10-inch loose-bottomed tart pan. Prick the bottom of the pastry case and chill 15-30 minutes longer.

Preheat the oven to 400°F with a baking sheet inside. Place the tart pan on the hot baking sheet and bake "blind" 15 minutes. Brush the pastry with the egg white and let cool. Reduce the oven temperature to 350°F.

Meanwhile, gently heat ½ cup sugar in 3½ cups water, stirring occasionally until dissolved, then bring to a boil. While the syrup is coming to a boil, peel, halve, and core the pears. Lower them into the boiling syrup and poach them about 5 minutes. Using a slotted spoon, transfer the pears to a bowl and sprinkle over the *poire Williams*. Let cool.

Beat together the butter and remaining sugar until light and fluffy, then gradually beat in the egg yolks. Lightly fold in the ground almonds and flour. Drain the liquid from the pears and stir 1½ tablespoons of it into the almond mixture. Pour this into the pastry case, reserving the remaining liquid. Arrange the pears on the almond mixture and press them down well. Bake in the oven about 15-20 minutes until the filling is lightly set and browned. When cooked, sprinkle over the reserved pear liquid, and serve the tart warm or cold.

BRIOCHE AU FROMAGE FRAIS DE CHÈVRE

(Illustrated on page 79)

SERVES 6-8
3 cups bread flour
pinch of salt
1 package quick-rise yeast
1-1½ tbsp milk
6oz fresh goat cheese or well-drained
fromage blanc
3 eggs, beaten
oil, for greasing bowl
butter, for greasing mold

Stir together the flour, salt, and yeast. Make a well in the center. Gradually stir the milk into the goat cheese or *fromage blanc*, followed by the eggs. Then add this to the well in the flour and gradually draw all the ingredients together. Turn onto a work surface and knead until you have a firm and elastic dough.

Place in a lightly oiled bowl, cover, and let rise until doubled in volume. Turn onto a lightly floured surface and punch down.

Break off one quarter of the dough and form it into a ball. Form the larger piece into a ball as well and place this in a buttered brioche mold. Set the smaller ball firmly on top. Alternatively, you can put the dough into the mold in one piece. Let rise again until the dough has doubled in volume.

Preheat the oven to 375°F. Bake the brioche about 30 minutes until it is golden and sounds hollow when tapped on the base. Cool in the mold a few minutes, then turn onto a wire rack.

LAND OF PLENTY

TOURAINE ALMOST IMPERCEPTIBLY BECOMES ANJOU: IN MANY WAYS, ESPECIALLY WHERE THE TWO REGIONS MERGE INTO EACH OTHER, ANJOU SEEMS LIKE A continuation of Touraine. It has a similar gentle climate and lovely green country, and is well endowed with orchards, market gardens, and vineyards. However, there are differences in the country, people, and the food, and each region has its own identity.

The Loire broadens as it approaches the end of its journey. Downstream from Angers, which is not actually on the Loire proper but on the Maine just before it flows into the Loire, one is aware that the sea is not too far away. On the uplands, away from the Loire, the landscape opens out into wide, lush green fields, and the sight of brown, brown-and-white, and black-and-white cows grazing contentedly serves to remind the visitor of the importance of cattle-raising to the economy of region.

(Opposite) A wonderful, lazy way to spend a day – whether fishing on the boat itself,
or idly watching from the bank.
(Above) Apples have been an important crop in Anjou for centuries, and are now big
business, because in recent years new pruning and cultivation techniques have
considerably increased yields.

1 *Flowers grown for cutting near Saumur.* **2** *Many small farms rear ducks for making foie gras and products such as confits.* **3** *Decorative ironwork on a gate near Saumur.* **4** *A hay barn on the road to Doué-la-Fontaine.* **5** *A hard-working country couple, still following the lifestyle of their forebears.* **6** *Painted panels in a boulangerie/pâtisserie in Angers.* **7** *The sight of many varieties of cabbage growing is a common one in Anjou, while a repertoire of magnificent cabbage dishes grace every table, from the humblest to the grandest.* **8** *Signs directing the way to homemade foie gras et ses dérivés can be seen around the countryside.* **9** *Strawberries are a lucrative crop in the Val-de-Loire. Sadly for the look of the countryside, they are often now grown under glass or in plastic tunnels.* **10** *Many Angevins consider shallots to be an essential flavoring in many a truly traditional regional recipe.* **11** *Apples on a market stall.*

1	2	3	4	5
6	7	8		
		9	10	11

(Overleaf)
NAPKINS
A restaurant's napkins are hung out to dry against a background of sunflowers.

FOIE GRAS
et ses dérivés
◄ici   L. Maudet

◄LA PETITE FERME

Nearer the river, the fields are smaller and surrounded by low walls of the characteristic white, soft, chalky, volcanic tufa, and the houses are topped by slated roofs. Slate was originally worked by open-cast methods from the sixteenth century onward. It was first mined in 1830, from subterranean galleries some 1,000 feet underground. Trélazé, near Angers, was once a world center of the slate industry.

Angevins are easy-going, with a relaxed attitude to time which can take a little getting used to – a *"quart d'heure Angevin"* is generally considered to last at least 30 minutes. As Anjou generally has a touch less culture than Touraine, and is not quite as sophisticated, the cooking is more homey and rural.

The Loire in Anjou also has its tributaries, although they are smaller than those in Touraine. To the north, there are the Oudon, the Mayenne, the Sarthe, and the Loir, which unite to form the Maine. To the south, there are the Layon, the Thouet, and the Dive, which join together south of Saumur. There are also some differences between the fish of the two regions. For example, perch, bream, and carp are Tourangeaux fish, while pike and shad are said to be better in Anjou than Touraine. Because they are nearer the sea and thus plumper (they do not feed on their way upstream), salmon fished from the Loire as it flows through Anjou are often thought superior to those caught in Tourangeaux waters.

Pike is gastronomically important in the Loire, and the most likely places to find it are the slack areas of the Loir, Thouet, and Aubance, and off the many small islands found in the Loire. Although an angler's favorite, its popularity with eaters has declined because of the multitude of small bones and the occasional muddy taste which occurs if the fish has been feeding in slow-moving or unclear waters and has not been flushed through thoroughly before cooking. Summer visitors should not expect too much if they try the local *brochet*, because the fish is at its best in the fall and early winter. At these times, the flavor of the lean, firm flesh can be good, although it may be a little dry and dull if the fish is large. For this reason, it is often puréed with cream to make *quenelles*, or served with rich sauces.

Unable to sleep one warm, starry night, I took a stroll by the Loire and almost literally stumbled across a fisherman. I am not sure which of us was more surprised, but he was the more loquacious as he gave vent to his irritation in a barely suppressed whisper. Realizing that the clumsy intruder was an Englishwoman interested in what he was doing – and in food – the other side of the true Frenchman took over and I was treated to a lengthy explanation of fishing together with a glass of his wine. Apparently fishing is not just the daytime activity I believed it to be, for it is not uncommon for local fishermen, along almost all of the region's rivers, to spend their nights peering through the darkness in quest of a shoal of the small fish that are the prey of the highly regarded pike-perch, or zander. As pike-perch can be farmed, do ask about its origins if you want to be certain of having the genuine Loire fish – the flavor of farmed fish lacks the distinction of that of the wild type.

In the spring, shad swim up the Loire from the sea to spawn. This is the time when the fish is most often served, as the roe is full and the time spent in fresh water has converted its

FRUIT TARTS
With a wide range of fruits, fillings, glazes, and recipes for pastry, and the innumerable computations of these, the number of different fruit tarts is legion.

flesh from being relatively ordinary to being plump and moist, with a delicious fine flavor. Shad is a member of the herring family, albeit a somewhat superior one. Indeed its firm white flesh has such a fine flavor that it is known as the "king of herrings." Shad does have two of the characteristics of herring which some people consider drawbacks: It is quite a rich fish (but these days we are being urged to eat oily fish for the sake of our hearts), and it contains a large number of small bones. The tradition of marrying shad with sorrel, either in the form of a purée or a stuffing, helps to negate both these problems. Sorrel has the ability to dissolve small bones, and its acidity counterbalances the fish's richness.

Spring is also the time to enjoy the eels which swim up the Loire, and along just about every other river in the area. Eels feed at any time of day or night on almost every kind of quatic creature, including fish. With a little cunning, therefore, it is relatively easy to catch one without a rod and line, although a fully grown eel is quite a handful. The canny Angevin practice is either to look carefully in likely places, such as roots of weed beds, overhanging clumps of weeds, twigs, and dead leaves, or to build an obstruction of twigs and weeds which will contain aquatic insects and encourage shoals of small fish to form. The obstruction is then lifted out of the water, and eels come with it. They are quickly extricated and placed on a sheet of newspaper spread out in expectation – this is the surest way of keeping eels still, the sticky adhesive effect of their mucous covering discouraging movement.

In the 2,600 miles of Angevin rivers, there are also plenty of small fry, such as gudgeon and bleak, for the fisherman's line and the cook's skillet.

Grown in the fertile land that stretches a mile or two on each side of the rivers are the fruits and vegetables which form the heart of Anjou cuisine. Both have become big business – but fruit is particularly successful. Some large companies are involved, and many growers have formed themselves into cooperatives. Much money and effort is put into tailoring the cultivation of fruit to the most appropriate areas, researching new varieties and crosses, reducing disease susceptibility, and improving handling and storage.

For a reminder that the fruit trade here is not a recent phenomenon, visit the village of Le Thoureil, near Gennes. This was once a river port from where locally grown apples were shipped, and the church tower had a light that guided the boats ashore on dark evenings.

Traditional standard trees have largely been replaced by espaliers as they make far better sense commercially. I don't think they make such an impressive sight when they are in bloom. Nevertheless, Anjou in the spring is glorious – there are even some signposted "blossom routes." Walking by the orchards, observing the differing shades, shapes, and densities of blossom is one of the most relaxing and revitalizing experiences I know. Throughout the season, there is a succession of colors, hues, and types of blossom, as different fruits and different varieties don their frilly spring outfits. This may be seen not only in the regimented orchards but in the hedgerows, which are dotted with white wild cherry, red hazelnut, and the occasional pink almond blossom.

The traditional Angevin *Prunus* fruits, such as plums, cherries, peaches, and apricots, are now not grown to the extent they were, because a greater, less troublesome, and more assured income can be earned from growing apples and pears, especially the former. *Prunus* flower early, so the buds are vulnerable to the late frosts which dog the region as late as the end of April; so where the trees are grown they tend either to be planted on slopes so the cold air will fall away, or trained in fans against a wall. The cold, dormant period every winter works to the benefit of the fruit, which has a good flavor as a result.

Apples flower later than pears, and the risk of late frost has been one of the reasons why apples have become the dominant fruit. Now it is hard to get away from late-flowering, heavy-cropping Golden Delicious ("Goldie") and Granny Smith ("Granny"). One fall when driving down to the Loire after about three years' absence, I saw a large billboard

POMMES TAPÉES

The process used today for preparing pommes tapées is the same as that used a century ago. The apples are peeled mechanically: about 40,000 cranks of the handle are needed to peel the 311 pounds that constitutes one oven load. The apples are laid out on large, flat wicker baskets, which are immersed in the Loire overnight to prevent them drying out too much during the 5 days of drying in the

ovens. Once dried, each apple is placed in a special mold and tapped with a purpose-built hammer about 20,000 times. Then they are sealed in jars.

Pommes tapées are usually eaten poached as a dessert, but they also go well with duck.

proclaiming a fair for "Granny and Goldie"; it took a little while before it dawned on me what the true subject of the weekend-long celebration was to be! Some of the easy-to-cultivate red varieties from the USA, such as Idared, are also being grown.

A honing down of varieties is also occurring with pears, with early-flowering and otherwise "difficult" varieties being phased out. One of these is the yellow, red-blushed Doyenné du Comice. It is a particular shame that this is disappearing; not only is it one of the best eating pears – with sweet, juicy, "buttery" flesh with a hint of spiciness and a harmonious blend of sweetness and acidity – but it originated in Angers. There is a gold-lettered plaque of Trélazé slate on a wall on the boulevard du Roi René to mark the site of the old garden of the nineteenth-century Comices Horticoles which reads: "In this garden/ was raised in 1849-50/the celebrated pear Doyenné du Comice/ by the gardener/ Dhommé and by Millet de la/Turtaudière/President of the Comices Horticoles." M. Millet de la Turtaudière had researched and worked very hard with single-minded dedication for years to produce the ultimate pear, Doyenné du Comice.

The Bon Chrétien pear (see page 69), which is called Bartlett in the USA and Williams in Great Britain, is easier to grow than Comice, but flowers earlier. The fruit is the first main variety to appear and can be eaten straight from the tree. It is large, and golden-yellow with a dash of russet, and its flesh is white, sweet, and juicy, with a musky note to the taste.

"Winter" pears (so called because they can be stored for a few months and are generally best for eating or cooking after storage) flower later than summer pears. They are more popular, with growers at least, and the region is the third largest producer in France. As well as Comice, varieties include the traditional plump, juicy, and sweet Beurré Hardy (named after a nineteenth-century director of the Luxembourg Gardens), the flesh of which, as the name implies, has a butter quality. It also has an intriguing, faint scent of rosewater. Like so many of the old favorites, however, the variety is being superseded by one preferred by growers – in this case, Passe-crassane. Fortunately, this is not the pear equivalent of Golden Delicious, and is a fat, juicy, rounded pear with a good flavor.

Such winter pears, and apples, would have been kept in well-ventilated cool, dry, cellars, individually wrapped in wax paper. Alternatively, they were made into *poires* or *pommes tapées* (see page 99) – especially processed whole dried fruits which were at first made domestically; but small-scale commercial production began in the mid-1880s after phylloxera created havoc in the vineyards, and *vignerons* needed an alternative source of income. A small group of them built special large ovens in the tufa caves at Turquant, on the banks of the Loire east

MARKET GARDENS
The favorable soil and climate makes small-scale vegetable and fruit growing on smallholdings and in gardens very rewarding. For those who sell their produce to local restaurants, it can also be profitable.

of Saumur. Production continued quite happily until around the turn of the century, then it began to decline and eventually died out. However, the practice was still carried out domestically in country areas until quite recently, and I have been told of people who still prepare *pommes tapées* in their own homes.

Today, it is possible to see the process in a refurbished troglodyte cave carved out of the tufa just east of Saumur. Alain Sylviane explained to me how he and his wife, Sylvie, discovered some caves containing some of the old ovens in their large backyard. They decided to revive the old custom and set about researching the method.

The region is also known for other fruits, such as strawberries. The light soil along the northern bank of the Loire between Saumur and Angers is particularly famed for its luscious, warmly-flavored berries. There is both quantity and quality in the region (it lies fourth in the league table of producers). Most are grown in open fields, but in response to fierce competition, increasing areas are being covered by glass or plastic tunnels, and new varieties of berries are being developed more with an eye to the color and handling and storage characteristics than flavor. However, fruit bursting with legendary old-fashioned flavor can be bought from small producers. There are also melons and raspberries, and black currants are grown alongside other crops because their season is so short, lasting just for the month of July. The currants tend to be exported to other regions of France, or used for liqueurs such as *crème de cassis* or *eau-de-vie*, or to make *pâte de cassis*.

The kitchen gardens and smallholdings producing vegetables have grown into increasingly larger market gardens, as growers and businessmen capitalize on the mild climate and fertile alluvial soil, coupled with good transport links and the proximity of lucrative Paris markets. This latter consideration has resulted in an emphasis on *primeurs*, which are grown particularly in the especially fertile stretch of land between the Loire and the Authion, just east of Angers – land which was drained, reclaimed, remodeled, and redistributed for cultivation between 1824 and 1832.

Asparagus is also an important crop. As in the Sologne, it thrives in a similar area to strawberries. Some of the country's best spears are grown in the light soil between Saumur and Angers, on the Angers side of the river, with Candé being a particularly famed site. Excellent artichokes also grow in the same general vicinity, as do fashionably-slim *haricots verts*, although different varieties of beans have been grown hereabouts for many years. These were not cooked *al dente* and served in neat bundles on elegant plates: Instead, they were dried, or half-dried, to provide a staple vegetable in winter. Around Saumur, *grenots* were – and still are – a particularly prized variety.

Cabbage is generally more in evidence, and Angevins are known affectionately in the local patois as "piochoux" (little cabbages). The region boasts arguably both the greatest number of recipes and the most varieties of cabbage, from the large *choux pommées*, down to small green *piochoux* or *piochons*. Not only do Angevins generally know how to cook cabbage to great advantage, but they can also cook each variety in the most suitable way. *Choux pommées* are blanched, then cooked slowly in a *cocotte* with sausages, while *piochons* are cooked in their own steam in a closed pot with just a little lightly salted butter. Butter is a favorite companion for cabbage, as in *fricassée de choux verts* and the local version of *chouée* (see page 138), which here is made from *piochons*, and may be called *darée de choux verts* – served with *beurre blanc* (see page 136) instead of plain butter, this really raises the profile of the humble cabbage. Butter also adds the final flourish to the simply delicious dish of *trompe-bonhomme*: Made from floury potatoes cooked in their skins (in the embers of the fire to be truly authentic), the peeled flesh is heaped on warm plates and eaten with plenty of good fresh, lightly salted butter, chopped shallot, and parsley.

Small white onions are also a feature of Angevin savory dishes, but the area is perhaps better known for its shallots. These are generally highly esteemed for their quality,

MUSHROOMS

Three-quarters of France's mushrooms come from Anjou's tufa caves, although more go to industrial processing than to market. The atmosphere and steady cool temperature of the caves are ideal for growing mushrooms, while the growers also benefit from low overheads. Around Saumur, the growers have an extra advantage in the proximity of the National School of Equitation which provides manure on which to grow the mushrooms. The mushrooms grown are psalliotes, or more familiarly

champignons de Paris, a relative of the common cultivated mushroom. I found the Loire mushrooms to have more flavor than most, for, characteristically in the Loire, a tastier type of psalliote is grown, the particular growing medium contributes greatly to the flavor, the mushrooms are left to grow a little longer so they develop a more mature taste, and the "root" is usually included when they are picked.

COINTREAU

The now-international liqueur firm of Cointreau has its roots in Angers. It was founded in 1849 by two brothers, Edouard and Adolphe Cointreau, who were confectioners and began experimenting with ways of using the abundant local fruit and alcohol. They also tried using the bitter orange peel arriving at Nantes from the West Indies, and hit upon the combination of this and matured spirit, which they

distilled and mixed with sugar syrup. Today, a mixture of dry bitter orange peels and fresh sweet peels, beet sugar, and alcohol is used – pure and simple, with nothing else added. Production is still carried out at Angers, in new premises on the outskirts, although the company's head office is in Paris.

especially the fairly small gray-brownish-skinned *échalote grise*. Anjou is, in fact, France's second largest producer of shallots, after only highly specialized and highly organized Brittany. Toward the west of the region, and more particularly where *primeurs* are grown, carrots, potatoes, leeks, and turnips begin to make an appearance.

In restaurants and private homes, I have frequently had the luck to be offered local fruit and nut *eaux-de-vie* and liqueurs. If these were homemade, they would usually be brought out of a cupboard with great pride; and no matter how nonchalantly the host drank his glassful, I knew my verdict was keenly awaited. Without exception, they have been good – often very good, with a quality that shows years of experience. This is only to be expected in any self-respecting area blessed with such an abundance of fruits and nuts; making alcoholic drinks is a most admirable way of using surpluses!

A record dating from 1693-1696 shows just how long *eaux-de-vie* and liqueurs have been produced in the area. It details a number of local *cabaretiers* (owners of bars where there was also entertainment) authorized to have a copper still for distillation in their house and to sell the *eau-de-vie* by "pot" (pitcher, tankard, or flagon). *Eaux-de-vie* were also sold by apothecaries and, illicitly, by *crieurs d'eau-de-vie* who went from door to door, they would set up their tables at street corners, complete with portable stills fueled by hand-lanterns, pewter flagons, and their cash registers. Everyone, including the authorities, knew this went on, but turned a blind eye. Suspect practices inevitably crept in, and one *eau-de-vie de poire* has gone down in local folklore for being "reinforced" with sulphuric acid.

Religious orders were also allowed to use stills, and in the first half of the seventeenth century, the Benedictine *Sœurs de Fidelité de Notre Dame du Bon Conseil* at Angers started producing what was to become a nationally renowned tipple. This was Guignolet, an *eau-de-vie* made from a number of cherries, such as wild, sour *griottes*, *merises*, and the small tart *guigne noir:* This was the indispensable element, as it gave the unique sharpness to the otherwise sweet drink. Each year the sisters made and sold many thousands of bottles.

After the disappearance of the priory in 1791, the making of Guignolet passed into the hands of *confiseurs*. Local peasants who picked the wild *guignes noirs* and sold them at their local market became known as *guignolets*. Production of the liqueur reached its peak in the nineteenth century, but tailed off toward the middle of this century. For some time now, the Anjou-based firm of Cointreau has been the only company producing it, and that in only a very small amount. Although *guignes noir* make very good *eau-de-vie* and liqueurs, being sharp they are not very good to eat, and many of the trees have been felled. However, some magnificent old trees remain, so it is worth keeping an eye open for the cherries. If you find some, prick them with a darning needle, put them into a bottle, add sugar to come one-quarter to one-third of the way up, pour in enough brandy to cover the fruit, seal firmly, and leave in a cool, dark place at least six months – preferably much longer.

Angers was the birthplace, in 1872, of the man who was given the title of the "prince of gastronomes." His real name was Maurice Edmond Sailland, but when he first started out in

journalism, he wanted a pen name to use for his articles. A friend suggested a Russian-sounding Latin name, "Cur-non-sky" (why-not-sky), which he adopted. He wrote copiously and intelligently on all culinary subjects, founded a monthly food-and-wine magazine, and set up the Académie des Gastronomes. Perhaps more than anyone else, he was also responsible for the great revival of interest in regional French food after the First World War. A friend of writers and fashionable people, an épicure, and a great host, fêted and feared by restaurateurs throughout France, he grew to weigh nearly 286 pounds and lived until he was 84. Until the end, he remained in love with his local cuisine and wines, but did not attempt to credit them with qualities that they did not possess. His words best sum up the food of the region: "... direct, reasonable, upright dishes which do not strive for effect." Anjou, he added, "is paradise for peaceful digestion."

VARNISHING THE BOATS
Traditional Loire boats are light and have a shallow draft – so they can easily be maneuvered off should they run aground on a recently formed shoal – and raised bows so they slide over obstructions in the riverbed.

CHEESES

Anjou does not have any cheeses of great – or indeed lesser – renown, except to a very local public. Nevertheless, visit a local market, such as the excellent Saturday morning market at Saumur, and you will see a mouthwatering range of local goat cheeses of varying sizes, shades, aromas, textures, and degrees of firmness. Frustratingly, they are also usually nameless. The reason for this anonymity is the number of very small goat-cheese producers. The cheeses they make, like most goat cheeses, will also be small.

Almost every rural family, even on really tiny properties, used to have one or two goats, because they are far more practical than a cow for a small plot of land, needing less space, and being easier to manage. Because goats produce less milk, there was little left over for cheese. The Loire's atmosphere and mild climate are also not ideal for keeping cheeses for any time, so they would usually be of a size that could be eaten at one sitting.

Many local residents will either have a favorite producer they visit in person (for some town dwellers, usually younger and more affluent, this is almost akin to the way in which many British families make their ritual Sunday pilgrimage to the countryside), or they will regularly visit the same stall at a market. A cheese so young and fresh that it is barely more than coagulated curds drained in a cheesecloth bag in a cool, airy place for a few hours, may perhaps be bought for eating the same day; for the next day, they may buy a slightly older and firmer cheese that has been given longer draining in faisselles, or other small molds. Older and firmer still are those cheeses that have been turned out of the molds and placed on straw or leaves on a cellar shelf and left just two to four weeks: goat cheeses lose moisture quickly, their flavor becoming more concentrated. Cheeses that are cendré are coated in the ashes of burned grapevine prunings. This coating slows down the maturation process and the cheese is slightly softer than an untreated version of the same age. Vine or nut leaves are also used occasionally.

WINES

There are some 1,000 vignerons in the region who depend entirely on the vine for their livelihood, and there are about 3,000 who may have just a few rows of vines as part of their overall farming, or other activity.

Although wines of a wide range of styles and quality are produced, to the public at large Anjou is best known for the light, sweetish, pink wines which account for about half of the region's wine production. There are, in fact,

AUTOMATIC REMUAGE

(Opposite, left)
AUTOMATIC REMUAGE
Wines made by the méthode champenoise undergo a second fermentation in the bottle. The bottles are rotated so the sediment produced moves down to the cork. This remuage used to be done manually, but machines, such as this one at Buvet-Ladubay, have taken over.

FOIE GRAS FARM

(Below)
FOIE GRAS FARM

three types of Anjou rosé. The most usual version is the medium-sweet Rosé d'Anjou. This is closely followed by Cabernet d'Anjou, also medium-sweet; because it is made from more "noble" grape varieties (cabernet franc and cabernet sauvignon), and production is more strictly controlled, it can age well. In 1974, the appellation Rosé de Loire was created to try to meet the demand for dry rosés, and these pale, salmon-colored, light wines can make pleasantly refreshing summer drinking when chilled.

However, production of the rosés is falling, especially that of the sweet "pop" style. In contrast, during the last 10 years the production of red wines has almost tripled and now equals the same 15 percent proportion of the total volume as sparkling wine. Anjou has some of the most dynamic and forward-looking vignerons of the Loire. Straight Anjou rouge can be made from gamay grapes or from the regionally more exciting cabernet franc. Whereas this latter grape variety is used on its own in Touraine, in Anjou it is combined with cabernet sauvignon to add backbone, structure, and finesse to the charming fruity flavors of the cabernet franc. The new generation of wine-makers is experimenting with the use of higher proportions of cabernet sauvignon, with the most up-to-date vinification techniques, and with aging wines in new oak casks (fûts de chêne neuf). Some will juggle with all of these practices; others will be more selective, so as to retain more of the wines' typicité. The enthusiastic oenocrats are also more likely to make more of selling their vieilles vignes wines (wines made from old vines), and even to use the ploy of separately vinifying and labeling their wines from young vines, and so by implication claiming a superiority.

The only place with a named red wine of any note is Saumur. The appellation Saumur rouge embraces quite a wide area, but the vineyards lying within the more closely delimited area of Saumur-Champigny, to the east of the town, yield a wine with greater class. The chalk soil of Saumur is suited to cabernet franc grapes, but here produces lighter wines with more immediate charm than those of a few miles away in Bourgueil and Chinon. Indeed, a good Saumur-Champigny can be one of the most lightly charming, eminently drinkable wines. Serve it chilled for ideal summer drinking, either on its own or as the perfect partner to most of the food of the region.

Reflecting the general trend in wine consumption, the move with ordinary Anjou blanc is now toward vinifying dry wines; 20 years ago, medium-sweet was the

GRATIEN & MEYER

Alfred Gratien founded his company in Saumur in 1864, at the same time as he formed Alfred Gratien Champagne in Épernay. Jean Meyer joined the company 6 years later. Although many sparkling Saumur houses are now owned by Champagne houses, Gratien & Meyer is the only one to have maintained unbroken links between the two districts for over 100 years. Also uniquely, it is entirely family owned and owns its own vineyards in the best crus above Saumur, yielding about 10 percent of the company's needs, the balance being bought in from nearby.

Gratien & Meyer produce only sparkling Saumur, using the same method as for Champagne. However, ebullient and charming Alain Seydoux, export director and direct descendant of Jean Meyer, believes that the way forward for sparkling Saumur producers is to market their wines as quality products in their own right, and so dispel the consumer perception of them as a poor man's Champagne.

vogue. Although the wines must contain at least 80 percent chenin blanc (locally known as pineau de la Loire), with the balance made up of chardonnay or sauvignon, they are not the best examples of what the grape can produce. A far better impression can be gained by tasting sparkling Saumur, the region's best-known white wine. It is produced in and around Saumur, using the méthode champenoise, although it will be illegal to put this on the label. It will, instead, be labeled "Saumur d'Origine."

It is not really meaningful to equate sparkling Saumur with Champagne because they are made from two distinct grape varieties grown on different soils in dissimilar climatic conditions, and so they will have quite unique flavors and styles. As with nearly every appellation of wine, there are good and bad examples of both. A good sparkling Saumur will have an elegant, "feminine," flowery-fruitiness, typical of the chenin blanc grape from which it is made. It may not just be white and dry, as sweet and red sparkling Saumur are also produced. An appellation for still white Saumur also exists.

The small area of Savennières, north of the Loire, is justly famous for its superb dry – occasionally semi-dry – white wines. Made from chenin blanc grapes to specifications of low yield and high natural alcohol, the wines from the thin, slatey soil are complex and not usually very attractive when young; they are, therefore, not wines for beginners. Given time (two to five years), however, the elements marry together and the wines blossom to a refined, elegant smoothness. They develop the characteristic chenin blanc bouquet, with its subtle, charming nuance of honey and flowers. There are two Savennières crus. Coulée de Serrant (see right) is the oldest, and has been planted with vines for six centuries, during which time its wines have often been highly praised. Curnonsky ranked it alongside Château d'Yquem. The other cru is La Roche-aux-Moines. The best vintages from each can last quite happily up to 50 years.

It will probably come as a surprise to all but the best informed wine drinkers to know that some of the Loire's – even, some claim, the world's – best sweet wines can be made in Anjou, when the weather has been kind in the summer and fall. They are produced from chenin blanc vines on the south-facing slopes in the Layon valley, and thus have the characteristic soft, fruity, floral-honeysuckle taste. They are also underpinned with quality-making acidity, which not only adds freshness to the flavor, but enables them to require a decade or more before they are ready for drinking.

The generic name for the sweet white wines of the area is Coteaux du Layon. These are rarely really lusciously sweet, so can accompany fish and poultry rather than sweet desserts. The best wines for this sort of use come from two crus. Quarts-de-Chaume, a small plot of just 125 acres has the lowest permitted yield per acre in France. When blessed with the right weather during the growing season, the reward for successive selective pickings of only the ripest grapes is a sumptuous golden wine, tasting of apricots, peaches, quinces, and honey. Bonnezeaux is a similar wine, but perhaps does not achieve quite the same heights.

CLOS DE COULÉE DE SERRANT

The small *appellation* of Coulée de Serrant was bought in 1960 by Madame Joly, who has worked extremely hard at reestablishing the quality and reputation of her wines. The vineyard has been managed according to the "biodynamic" system since 1985. This rejects the use of chemicals, and also advises against the use of clonally-bred vines. In addition, the Joly's wines are vinified completely naturally. Add to

this restrictive program the low yield permitted under AOC regulations, and one can see why Coulée de Serrant wines are never cheap.

(Left)
ANJOU VINEYARDS NEAR THE RIVER LAYON

SOUPE DES PÊCHEURS

Fishermen's Soup

SERVES 6

4 lb mixed freshwater fish, such as carp, pike,
catfish, whitefish, perch, etc.
a fresh, bouquet garni consisting of 4 sprigs of
parsley, 2 sprigs of thyme, 1 small bay leaf,
3 sprigs of chervil, and 2 sprigs of tarragon
1 onion, sliced
2 carrots, chopped
2 leeks, sliced
2 cups dry white Loire wine
salt and freshly ground black pepper
3 egg yolks
1 cup crème fraîche
finely chopped fresh herbs, for garnish

Have the fish drawn, reserving the heads
and tails. Put these trimmings into a large
pot with the bouquet garni, vegetables,
wine, and 2 cups of water. Bring to a boil,
skim the scum from the surface, and then
simmer 20 minutes, skimming occasionally.

Cut the fish into 1½-inch pieces.

Strain the stock and season. In a clean
pan, gently heat the stock just to a simmer.
Add the fish in the order given, allowing
the liquid to return to a simmer between
each addition. Poach the fish 10 minutes,
or until just tender. Using a slotted spoon,
transfer the fish to a warmed soup tureen
and keep warm. Boil the cooking liquid
until reduced by half.

Blend together the egg yolks and crème
fraîche, then stir in a little of the cooking
liquid. Pour this mixture into the saucepan and heat very gently, stirring, until
slightly thickened; do not allow to boil.
Taste for seasoning, then pour the sauce
over the fish. Garnish with the herbs.

TARTE À LA TOMATE

Tomato Quiche

(Illustrated left)

This is an adaptation of Mme Harrault's
delicious quiche from Le Chapy (see far
right). Its special appeal depends upon
plump, juicy, and well-flavored tomatoes,
which need no greengrocer's sign
proclaiming them "freshly picked" as their
smell makes this all too obvious.

SERVES 8

FOR THE PÂTE BRISÉE
1⅔ cups flour
1 stick butter
2 egg yolks

FOR THE FILLING
2 egg yolks, beaten, plus egg white for brushing
4 tbsp unsalted butter, diced
2 large onions, chopped
salt and freshly ground black pepper
⅔ cup crème fraîche
2-3 tsp chopped fresh herbs
6 large, well-flavored, ripe-but-firm tomatoes,
skinned if wished and sliced
⅔ cup shredded Cantal cheese

Make the pâte brisée with the flour, butter,
egg yolks, and 4 tablespoons of water as
on page 77, and chill for 30 minutes.

Roll out the pastry dough and use it to
line a 12- x 9-inch quiche pan or baking
dish. Chill again about 30 minutes.

Preheat the oven to 400°F with a baking
sheet inside. Prick the bottom of the pastry
case, place it on the hot baking sheet, and
bake "blind" about 15 minutes. Remove
from the oven, brush with the egg white
and let cool. Reduce the oven temperature
to 350°F.

Melt the butter in a skillet over low heat.
Add the onions and cook very gently,

stirring occasionally, until very soft. Using a slotted spoon, transfer the onions to a bowl to cool. Stir together the egg yolks, crème fraîche, and seasoning. Stir in the onions and herbs, then pour this mixture into the pastry case. Arrange the tomato slices on top. Sprinkle with the cheese and bake about 20-25 minutes.

Serve warm or cold.

SALADE DE GRENOTS À L'HUILE DE NOIX

White Beans with Walnut Oil

There are many wild walnut trees in the Anjou area. The tufa soil gives a very special taste to the walnuts and, therefore to the oil made from them. This is an old family recipe of the 150-year-old firm, Huilerie Croix-Verte in Saumur.

SERVES 4
2 cups grenots or other dried white beans, soaked overnight
a bouquet garni
1 tbsp unsalted butter
2 shallots, preferably gray, chopped
about ¼ cup walnut oil
salt and freshly ground black pepper
chopped parsley, for garnish

Drain the beans and rinse them in fresh water. Put them in a pot, add the bouquet garni, cover with water, and bring to a boil. Boil 10 minutes, then cover and simmer 1-1½ hours, depending on the freshness of the beans (the fresher the beans, the shorter the cooking time). Make sure there is adequate water.

Meanwhile, melt the butter in a sauté pan, add the shallots, and cook 2-3 minutes only: They should retain some crunch. Drain the beans, discard the bouquet garni, and stir into the shallots. Toss with walnut oil and seasoning to taste. Sprinkle with chopped parsley and serve warm.

ŒUFS POCHÉS SAUMUROIS

Poached Eggs in White Wine

SERVES 4
4 tbsp unsalted butter
½ cup chopped mushrooms
⅔ cup chopped onions
1 ¼ cups dry white Saumur wine
¾ cup stock
1 sprig of fresh tarragon
4 eggs
salt and freshly ground black pepper
4 slices of hot toasted country bread, buttered, to serve

Melt half of the butter in a heavy-based saucepan. Add the mushrooms and onions and cook over very low heat about 10 minutes, until softened, without allowing to color. Add the dry white wine, stock, and tarragon and simmer 10 minutes. Strain off the liquid into a bowl, and keep the mushroom mixture warm in another bowl.

Return the liquid to the pan and reheat to just below simmering point. Add the eggs and poach until the yolks are set almost to the required degree of doneness. Using a slotted spoon, remove the eggs and dry them briefly on paper towels. Keep warm.

Boil the liquid until slightly syrupy. Lower the heat and gradually whisk in the remaining butter. Season. Place the mushroom mixture on the toast, place the eggs on top, and pour the sauce over them.

LE CHAPY
Allonnes
Tel 41 52 02 63
See recipe opposite

Annick and Jean-Claude Harrault have farmed their land 2½ miles from Allonnes close to Saumur for 25 years. More rural it couldn't be, with free-range ducks and chickens, sheep, and a huge area for growing vegetables and fruit, including tomatoes, beans, strawberries, raspberries, melons, potatoes, and corn. In 1985, Mme Harrault opened Le Chapy, inspired by years of praise for her cooking from friends, and putting into practice all the knowledge learned from her grandmother and mother. Don't be fooled by the rather rustic-looking signs to Le Chapy: they greatly belie the quality of the *cuisine familiale* found there.

Pois à la Mode de l'Abbaye Fontevraud

Peas with Lettuce Hearts and Cream

At the side of Fontevraud Abbey, there is an unusual squat structure built on a *quadratum* of 4 corner towers with a large central tower, all topped by pepper-pot roofs. These towers are the chimneys for the five separate hearths in the kitchen beneath, where the food was cooked for the Abbey's 500 or so residents.

When cooking peas this way I like to reflect upon the tranquillity of the Abbey's interesting old vegetable garden; I can imagine the frugal cooks devising a recipe that works just as well for old peas as young ones, and wrapping the just-shelled peas in a damp napkin to keep them fresh.

SERVES 4-6
3 cups shelled peas
1 head of Boston lettuce, outside leaves removed
1 sprig of fresh summer savory (optional)
salt and freshly ground white pepper
1-2 sticks unsalted butter
1 egg yolk
¾ cup crème fraîche
pinch of sugar (optional)

Wrap the peas in a damp napkin. Open out the lettuce head and place the sprig of summer savory, if used, between the leaves. Tie up the lettuce and put it in a heavy pot with the peas, a pinch of salt, the butter, and 6 tablespoons of water. Simmer until the peas are just tender.

Blend the egg yolk with the crème fraîche, pepper, and sugar, if used.

Remove the lettuce from the pot. Blend the cream mixture into the peas and heat gently; do not allow to boil.

Ragoût d'Artichauts Saumurois

Artichokes with Mushrooms
(*Illustrated opposite, left*)

This dish brings together two of the area's best-known foods. Artichokes are clearly visible for all to see, while the area's mushrooms are hidden away in tufa caves (see page 103). The flavor of the result belies the simplicity of the recipe. Possible additions include tender, sweet young peas or fava beans added after 15 or 12 minutes cooking respectively, or cooked fresh shrimp, stirred in at the end and allowed just to heat through.

SERVES 4
4-8 globe artichokes, depending on size
juice of 1 large lemon
1 tbsp white wine vinegar
2 tbsp unsalted butter
¼ cup dry white non-sparkling Saumur wine
salt and freshly ground black pepper
¼lb fresh crèpes, fairly thinly sliced
few sprigs of fresh chervil, chopped, for garnish

Break off the artichoke stems close to their bases.

Pull away and discard the first few outer layers of leaves from one artichoke. Using a large, sharp, stainless steel knife, cut across this artichoke about halfway down. Using a small, sharp, stainless steel knife, trim away all the leaves. Cut or pull away the inner leaves and pull away the hairy choke, leaving just the tender base.

Brush the base with lemon juice, then put it into water acidulated with the wine vinegar. Prepare the remaining artichokes in the same way.

Take the artichokes out of the water one by one and cut each base into quarters, sixths, or eighths, depending on size. Brush the cut surfaces with lemon juice.

Melt the butter in a saucepan and add the artichokes and wine. Season lightly, cover partly, and cook over low heat about 20 minutes, tossing frequently, until the artichokes are nearly tender. Add the mushrooms and cook 5 minutes longer. Check the seasoning.

Transfer to a warmed serving dish and sprinkle with the chervil.

Chou au Beurre

Buttered Cabbage
(*Illustrated opposite, right*)

This is quite unlike the usual concept of cabbage with butter – over-boiled cabbage with a pat of butter on top. It takes time to do the buttering, but it is worth every minute. The cabbage retains its bright-green color and reduces considerably to a delicious result.

SERVES 4
1 small head of Savoy or other green cabbage
4 tbsp unsalted butter, diced
salt and freshly ground black pepper

Cut the cabbage into strips and remove the core. Cook in boiling salted water 7-8 minutes until just tender. Drain thoroughly.

Melt half of the butter in the same pan, return the cabbage to it, and stir over low heat. As the liquid from the cabbage is produced and re-absorbed, gradually add the remaining butter, stirring gently.

When the cabbage is thoroughly coated with butter, and there is no remaining liquid, add plenty of black pepper, but not too much salt. Serve immediately.

SANDRE FARCI, SAUCE À L'ANJOU ROUGE

Stuffed Pike-Perch with a Sauce of Red Anjou Wine

Paul Le Quéré of Pavillon Paul Le Quéré (see page 117) kindly gave me this recipe.

SERVES 6
1 tbsp olive oil
½ smallish fennel bulb, chopped
1¾ cups finely chopped mushrooms
about 5oz sorrel, trimmed
salt and freshly ground black pepper
6 thick slices of pike-perch fillet
1½ sticks unsalted butter, chopped
3 shallots, preferably gray, finely chopped
1¾ cups red Anjou wine
melted butter for brushing

(Above)
Slices of pike-perch as served in red wine sauce at the Pavillon Paul Le Quéré, with a garnish of zucchini and other seasonal vegetables, and with onion leaves slowly cooked in red Anjou wine sweetened with honey.

Heat the olive oil in a skillet over low heat and gently cook the fennel in it until softened. Add the mushrooms and sorrel and cook over low heat, stirring occasionally, about 10 minutes. Season, then let cool.

Cut horizontally through each piece of fish fillet, and place the sorrel stuffing in between the two layers.

Melt 2 tablespoons of the butter in a heavy-based pan over a low heat and cook the shallots in it, stirring occasionally, until softened. Add the wine and simmer until reduced to about 6 tablespoons. Over low heat, gradually whisk in the remaining butter. Season to taste. Keep warm over very low heat, but do not allow to boil.

Season the top of each piece of fish, and brush with melted butter. In a nonstick skillet over moderate-to-high heat, cook the fish 2 minutes on each side, turning the pieces over carefully. Transfer to 6 warmed plates and spoon the sauce over.

FRITURE

Deep-fried Small Fish
(Illustrated right)

Friture was a popular dish with boatmen along the Loire, and is still sold in small cafés and restaurants along the banks of the river. The best friture will be found in establishments supplied with freshly-caught small fish. In spring, these fish would include gudgeon and smelts, which swarm into fresh water to spawn, small perch (*perchettes*), and bleak, abundant in the Loire and its tributaries. In some popular places, friture may be no more than what would elsewhere be termed *goujons*, or strips of fish, rather than small fishes.

The fish are coated in milk and flour, then dipped twice in hot oil: The first time cooks the fish, the second crisps it up. They should be eaten very soon after the second cooking, while they are very hot and "crackling." The fish will lose their crispness quite quickly, so it is best not to cook for too many people eating at the same time. Fried parsley is tradition-ally tossed with the fish, and you must work quickly if everything is to be at its delicious best. At Notre Dame (see page

118), where this photograph was taken, M. Choupin served the *friture* with sliced tomatoes and chopped shallots mixed with the parsley.

The following recipe makes a light main course or delightful first course, and the crisp, dry style that typifies white Loire wines is the ideal vinous accompaniment.

SERVES 4
clean flavorless oil, for deep-frying
flour, for coating
salt and freshly ground black pepper
1½lb very fresh small fish, drawn if liked
about ¾ cup milk
small handful of fine parsley sprigs
lemon wedges, to serve

Heat a good depth of oil to 350°F. Season some flour with salt and pepper. Dip the fish in milk, allowing the excess to drain off, then toss a few at a time in a bag containing the seasoned flour, to coat them lightly and evenly. Keep the different types of fish separate.

Carefully lower a few fish at a time into the hot oil and cook briefly until it is lightly colored. Keep the cooked fish warm while cooking the remaining fish, and keep an eye on the temperature of the oil to make sure that it does not drop.

When all the fish have been cooked once, reheat the oil, and plunge the fish back in to crisp them up and turn them golden. Remove the pan from the heat. Lift the fish out onto paper towels to drain.

Using a slotted spoon, lower the parsley sprigs into the oil and fry about 8-10 seconds. Then scoop them out with the slotted spoon and drain on paper towels.

Sprinkle the fish with salt, toss with the parsley, and serve with lemon wedges.

FRICASSÉE DE POULET ANGEVINE

Chicken in White Anjou Wine

SERVES 4

3½-lb free-range chicken, cut into 4 portions
4 tbsp unsalted butter
16 small onions
1 cup chicken stock
1 cup dry white Anjou wine
a small bouquet garni
salt and freshly ground white pepper
12 medium-sized mushrooms, wiped and halved
2 egg yolks
juice of ½ lemon

In a Dutch oven, melt the butter over medium heat. Add the onions and the chicken pieces, skin-side down, and cook about 10 minutes without allowing to color, turning the chicken over halfway. Remove and reserve the onions. Add the stock, wine, bouquet garni, and seasoning to the chicken. Cover and cook over low heat about 20 minutes. Add the onions and cook 20 minutes longer, until the chicken is just cooked. Add the mushrooms and cook 10 minutes.

Remove the chicken, mushrooms, and onions from the pot, cover, and keep warm. Skim excess fat from the surface of the cooking liquid, then boil it until reduced by about one-quarter.

Remove a ladleful of this liquid and let it cool slightly, then stir it into the egg yolks. Pour back into the pot and heat, stirring constantly, until slightly thickened; do not allow to boil. Add the lemon juice and adjust the seasoning. Return the chicken, mushrooms, and onions to the pot and turn them over to coat them in the sauce.

PINTADEAU SUR NOIX

Guinea Fowl with Walnuts

The black-and-white speckled plumage of guinea fowl can still be seen in country gardens and on smallholdings in the area – a reminder that, in France, the birds were part of the farmyard flock. They have a much better flavor than we tend to expect, although that of true corn-fed chickens is almost as good.

This recipe comes from a family that has kept guinea fowl for as long as any of them could remember – and the gnarled form of the walnut tree in their garden is witness to the family's longevity. The cheese for the stuffing also used to be homemade, but is no longer.

Inserting a stuffing between the skin and the meat of the breast, and perhaps the legs, of a bird has become fashionable in recent years, but it is no surprise that such an obviously good idea has been in use for a long time.

SERVES 3-4

5-oz piece of lightly smoked bacon, cut across into strips
½ cup soft full-fat cream cheese
¼ cup skinned and chopped walnuts, preferably fresh
2 small shallots, chopped
salt and freshly ground black pepper
1 plump guinea fowl, dressed
2 tbsp walnut oil
6-8 walnut or grape leaves
6 tbsp good dry white Saumur wine
sprigs of fresh chervil, for garnish
½ cup walnut halves, tossed in hot butter

Preheat the oven to 375°F.

Heat a Dutch oven over fairly low heat, add the bacon, and cook until the fat runs, without allowing it to color. Remove the pot from the heat and scoop out about one-quarter of the bacon. Drain on paper towels and chop or crumble.

Mix with the cream cheese, nuts, 1 tablespoon of shallot, and seasoning. Season the cavity of the guinea fowl, then insert the stuffing in between the meat and skin of the breast and over the legs.

Return the Dutch oven to the heat, stir in the remaining shallot, and cook, stirring occasionally, until softened.

Rub walnut oil liberally over the guinea fowl skin, then tie walnut or grape leaves over the back and breast.

Pour the wine into the pot, allow it to bubble briefly, and then place the bird, breast-side down, in the pot. Cover tightly and cook in the oven 35 minutes. Turn the bird so that the breast is uppermost, cover the pot again, and cook 30 minutes or so longer, until the guinea fowl is just cooked through.

Transfer the guinea fowl to a warmed plate. Check the seasoning of the cooking juices. Surround the guinea fowl with butter-tossed walnuts, spoon the sauce over the bird, and garnish with chervil.

Serve accompanied by more of the Saumur, or a Saumur-Champigny.

"L'ÉTUVE" D'AGNEAU DE LAIT

Lamb with Young Loire Vegetables
(Illustrated opposite)

This is an adaptation of a dish created by Paul Le Quéré of Pavillon Paul Le Quéré (see far right) both to show off local produce to advantage, and to produce a dish which is fundamentally old-fashioned cuisine du terroir but modern in execution.

The mélange of vegetables chosen for the garnish will vary according to what is particularly good on any given day, bearing in mind that it must be complementary to the fine, delicate flavor of the lamb.

SERVES 6
3½lb young lamb chops and chopped fillet end of leg
leaves from 3 sprigs of rosemary, chopped
leaves from 3 small sprigs of fresh thyme, chopped
½ cup olive oil
1 stick + 6 tbsp unsalted butter
3 shallots, chopped
4 large tomatoes, skinned, seeded, and chopped
2 cups light veal stock
salt and freshly ground black pepper
¼-½ cup chopped fresh herbs such as basil, thyme, tarragon, flat-leaf parsley, chives, and chervil, plus more for garnish
seasonal vegetables, for garnish

Place the lamb in an earthenware terrine, and add the rosemary and thyme and 6 tablespoons of the oil. Cover with a lid or foil and leave in a cool place 2 hours.

Lift the lamb from the marinade. Heat the remaining oil and 2 tablespoons of the butter in a large sauté pan. Add the lamb and brown it evenly, about 5 minutes. Transfer the lamb to a warmed plate and keep warm.

Pour off the fat from the pan. Add another 2 tablespoons of butter and the shallots and cook 2 minutes. Stir in the tomatoes, cook 1 minute, and then add the stock. Simmer about 10 minutes. Gradually whisk in the remaining butter, adjust the seasoning, and add the chopped mixed herbs. Add the lamb and the vegetables for the garnish to the sauce, heat about 1 minute, and then serve, sprinkled with more herbs.

PAVILLON PAUL LE QUÉRÉ
3 boulevard Foch
Angers
Tel 41 20 00 20
See recipes on pages 114, 123, and left

When Martine and her chef-patron husband Paul Le Quéré had their restaurant, "Le Quéré," in Angers, they gained a reputation for the finest cooking in the area, and for offering the best and widest selection of Loire wines (these were the domain of highly respected sommelier Martine). However, the surroundings were not in the same league, so the couple felt that if they were to join the highest echelons of top restaurants they would have to move. After a long search they settled for a secluded but neglected listed building right in the heart of Angers. Given extensive renovation, the Pavillon Paul Le Quéré has become not only a luxurious restaurant, but has a few well-appointed guest rooms, too. Martine is now involved with administration, as well as keeping an eye on all the work that is carried out both "behind the scenes" and "front of house." Paul is continuing the policies of using local ingredients, specializing in Loire fish, and giving precise consideration to matching all his dishes to wines on their extensive wine list.

NOTRE DAME

Place de l'Église
Béhuard
St-Georges-sur-Loire
Tel 41 72 20 17
See recipe on pages 114-15 and
picture opposite

At about 2 miles long and with
94 residents, the island of
Béhuard is one of the largest on
the Loire, and also one of its
most attractive and interesting,
with verdant pastures, country
lanes as they should be, and
peaceful avenues of poplars
gliding down to the river's edge.
At the heart is the pre-Christian
village of St-Georges-sur-Loire.
A number of restaurants cluster
in or near the main square, but
the simple family restaurant of
Notre Dame, run by the
husband-and-wife team of
Giselle and Gérard Choupin, is
the one famed for its *fritures*.
Depending on your mood, and
the side of French life you want
to see and be a part of, you can
either eat in the bar or dine
more quietly in the restaurant.

MATELOTE DES TONNELIERS

Veal Casseroled in Wine

Matelote in this instance means "cooked in wine." The wine used here is red to make a richly-flavored casserole from veal to satisfy hungry *tonneliers*, the men who transported wine on the Loire. Saumur-Champigny has quite a delicate flavor; you can substitute a Cabernet d'Anjou for greater robustness.

SERVES 4
5 tbsp butter, diced
16 small onions
2 small carrots, chopped
¾lb boneless shoulder of veal, cut into
1½inch cubes
¾lb boneless breast of veal, cut into cubes along
the direction of the grain
2 tsp plain flour
1¾ cups Saumur-Champigny wine
a fresh bouquet garni consisting of 2 sprigs of
thyme, 1 bay leaf, 2 sprigs of parsley, and a sprig
of chervil
salt and freshly ground black pepper

Melt half of the butter in a sauté pan or large shillet, add the vegetables, and cook over low heat about 5 minutes.

Stir in the veal and cook 2-3 minutes. Sprinkle with the flour, stir 2-3 minutes, and then gradually stir in the wine. Add the bouquet garni. Bring just to a simmer, then cover tightly and cook gently about 1 hour, or until the meat is very tender.

Uncover the pan toward the end of cooking, if necessary, to evaporate some of the liquid. If, by the time the veal is tender, there is still too much liquid, strain it off and boil it until well reduced and concentrated. Discard the bouquet garni, adjust the seasoning, and stir in the remaining butter to finish.

CUL DE VEAU À L'ANGEVINE

Loin of Veal in Anjou or Saumur wine

In Anjou, *cul de veau* is the *quasi-entier*, that is, the whole hind loin plus the rump, but as this makes a rather large amount I have used a smaller cut. If pork skin proves impossible to find, the dish can be made without, it but the sauce will lose much of its delicious unctuousness.

SERVES 6
1 large piece of fresh pork skin
2 onions, chopped
3 small carrots, chopped
3-lb veal loin roast
1 cup dry white Anjou or Saumur wine
¾ cup veal stock
a fresh bouquet garni, of 2 sprigs of thyme, ½ bay
leaf, 1 sprig of chervil, 6 chives, and 1 sprig
of parsley
½ cup crème fraîche
salt and freshly ground black pepper

Preheat the oven to 400°F.

Line the bottom of a Dutch oven with the pork skin, fat-side down. Layer the onions and carrots on the skin. Season the veal roast and set it on the vegetables. Place, uncovered, in the oven and cook 20 minutes, turning the roast over halfway through. Add the wine, stock, and bouquet garni.

Cover tightly and continue cooking, about 1½ hours, turning the meat over 2 or 3 times.

Remove the veal, cover, and keep warm. Discard the pork skin, vegetables, and bouquet garni. Strain the cooking liquid and skim off excess fat. Bring the liquid to a boil and reduce to concentrate the flavor. Stir in the crème fraîche and simmer until thickened. Adjust the seasoning to taste.

Carve the veal into thick slices, arrange them overlapping on a warmed plate, and pour the sauce over the meat. Or carve the veal at the table and serve the sauce separately in a warmed gravy boat.

(Above)
Wines for the Saumur appellations are grown on the south side of the Loire. The best known are the Champagne-style white wines, and the charming red Saumur-Champigny, their areas of production being separated by the town of Saumur: The red wines are produced east of the town, the white ones to the west.

(Left)
Gérard Choupin cooked his version of carré de veau for us at his restaurant, Notre Dame (see opposite). For his recipe, the veal and vegetables are fried to a rich brown before braising in wine and stock; to create such a dark sauce, red wine would, of course, be used.

SAUTÉ DE PORC AUX PRUNEAUX

Pork with Prunes

(Illustrated right)

Ever since Alain Seydoux of Gratien &
Meyer (see page 107) demonstrated to me
the excellence of the partnership between
a sparkling *demi-sec* white Saumur wine
and *porc aux pruneaux*, I always serve the
two together.

Porc aux pruneaux is one of the best-
known dishes of the *Val de Loire*, and
there are many versions. This one is based
on a recipe from M. Timmerman, a
Saumurois *traiteur*, who often cooks it for
the guests of Gratien & Meyer when the
company entertains in its private dining
rooms in the cellars. It is my favorite, because it is akin to traditional family recipes,
particularly in not including cream. Use
large prunes that need soaking, because
those that do not have been treated. M.
Timmerman adds a garnish of carefully
prepared seasonal vegetables.

SERVES 4
16-20 large prunes
1 bottle dry white Saumur wine
2 tbsp butter
2½lb very lean boneless shoulder of pork, chopped
2 cups chopped mixed carrot, onion, and celery
a fresh bouquet garni consisting of 2 sprigs of
parsley, 1 bay leaf, and 3 sprigs of thyme
1 cup veal stock
salt and freshly ground black pepper
a little lemon juice

Put the prunes in a bowl, cover with half
of the wine, and soak overnight.

Melt the butter in a sauté pan, add the
pork, and brown it lightly on all sides.

Drain on paper towels, then place in
a Dutch oven. Add the vegetables and
bouquet garni to the pot.

Stir the remaining wine into the sauté
pan, bring to a boil, and then pour onto
the pork. Add the stock. Season, cover
tightly, and cook over low heat about 1½
hours. Add the prunes and their soaking
liquid, cover again, and cook 30 minutes
longer.

Transfer the pork and prunes to a
serving dish, cover, and keep warm. Boil
the cooking liquid until slightly thickened.
Taste and adjust the seasoning, adding a
little lemon juice if necessary, then press
through a strainer over the pork and
prunes. I strongly recommend a *demi-sec*
sparkling white Saumur wine with this.

PIGEONNEAU ET PETIT CHOU FARCI

Squab with Small Cabbage Rolls

Serge Lebert, *chef-patron* of Le Clafoutis,
just outside Angers, gave me this wonderfully savory, typical country Angevin
recipe, He used Coteaux de l'Aubance
wine (a sweet wine from chenin blanc
grapes) from south of the Loire. Production of this wine is small and it is rarely
found outside the area, so he suggested
using Coteaux du Layon instead. Bread is
the only accompaniment necessary.
Game birds such as partridge or pheasant
could be used, but wild pigeon is the traditional choice.

SERVES 4
8 smallish cabbage leaves
5 tbsp unsalted butter
2/3 cup chopped shallots
4 young squab pigeons, dressed weight of each
about 1lb, hearts, livers, and giblets reserved
1½ cups Coteaux de l'Aubance, or similar
medium-dry Anjou white wine
salt and freshly ground black pepper
7oz good-quality pork sausage meat
1 egg, beaten
1 tbsp chopped fresh chives
1 piece of caul fat (optional)
½-lb piece of slab bacon, diced
1 cup chopped onions
1½ cups chopped carrots
2 sprigs of fresh thyme
1 bay leaf
2 cups chicken stock

Preheat the oven to 375°F.

Blanch the cabbage leaves in boiling salted water 2 minutes. Drain, refresh under cold running water, drain well again, and let dry and cool on paper towels or a clean dishtowel.

Melt 1 tablespoon of butter in a heavy-based saucepan and add the shallots and finely chopped squab giblets, if available. Cook gently 2-3 minutes. Stir in ¼ cup of the wine, then boil until reduced. Season and mix with the sausage meat, egg, and chives.

Spread out the cabbage leaves and cut out the central veins. Divide the stuffing among the leaves. Fold the leaves over to make neat rolls, then wrap these in the caul, if available.

Melt 2 tablespoons of butter in a Dutch oven into which the cabbage rolls will just fit, and add half of the bacon, and half the onions and carrots. Cook, stirring occasionally, until lightly browned. Pack the cabbage rolls on top, making sure the seams are underneath. Tuck in the herbs, and pour in ¾ cup of the wine and sufficient stock to come just over halfway up the parcels. Cook on the lower rack of the oven for about 40 minutes. After this time, pour off and reserve the cooking liquid.

Meanwhile, rub the squabs with some of the remaining butter, season, and put in a roasting pan on the rack above the cabbage, basting from time to time, about 15 minutes. Remove the breasts and legs from the squabs and keep warm. Chop the carcasses and return them to the roasting pan with the remaining onions and carrots and brown lightly on top of the stove. Stir in the remaining wine and boil until almost evaporated, then stir in the liquid from the cabbage. Boil until slightly thickened. Strain the sauce, reheat, and gradually swirl in the remaining butter. Adjust the seasoning.

Transfer the cabbage rolls, carrots and onions to warmed plates, add the squab breasts and legs, and pour the sauce over the top.

(Above)
Onions put by among a jumble of old-fashioned agricultural tools and implements (all probably still in use, and valued for their original purposes) will eventually be used to add savor to winter cooking.

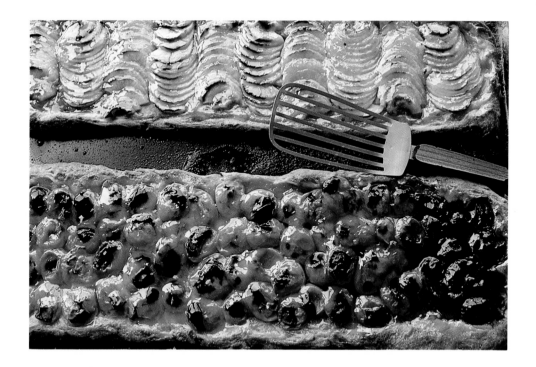

15-30 minutes. Preheat the oven to 400°F. Bake the pastry case "blind" about 10 minutes, until lightly colored.

Arrange the fruit in the pastry case. Return to the oven and bake until the fruit is almost tender. Sprinkle with sugar to taste, then bake about 5 minutes longer until the sugar melts and glazes the surface. Serve warm or cold.

COUPE DE FRAISES

Strawberries in Wine

The luscious Angevin strawberries, which ripen to bright fruitiness in the clear, warm sunlight of the area, marry to perfection with the many styles of good Anjou wines: crystal-honeyed white wines of the Coteaux du Layon; red wines with low tannin levels and plenty of soft fruit typified by Saumur-Champigny; and sparkling wines to suit all tastes – dry, *demi-sec*, sweet, and a light sweetish red that makes a surprisingly good match for the berries. The end result will vary according to the style of wine.

SERVES 4
1½ pints ripe strawberries
sugar (optional)
1 bottle sparkling Saumur wine, chilled, or about
1¼ cups still white or red wine

Hull the strawberries and sprinkle with a little sugar unless a sweet wine is used.

If using sparkling wine, pour enough over the berries almost to cover them. Cover and chill lightly. Then divide the strawberries among 4 goblets and pour in more wine almost to cover.

If using still wine, pour the wine over the berries, cover and keep in a cool place for about 2 hours, then chill.

TARTE AUX MIRABELLES

Mirabelle Tart

(Illustrated above)

Château de la Jaillière near Angers has belonged to the d'Anthènaise family for hundreds of years. In the grounds there is the most idyllic walled fruit garden – a real haven of sun, fruit, vegetables, and herbs – from where the present countess picked the small sublime mirabelles for the *tarte* she had prepared as the finale to our lunch.

This recipe for a glazed tart can be used with any suitable fruit. For a classic apple tart, peel, core, and thinly slice sweet apples and arrange them generously, in neat overlapping rows, in the pastry case, as shown above. Peaches make an equally delicious tart.

SERVES 6-8
1½ cups plain flour
pinch of salt
7 tbsp unsalted butter, chopped
1½ tbsp vanilla-flavored sugar
1¼-1½lb mirabelle greengage plums, halved
and pitted
sugar, for sprinkling

Sift the flour and the salt into a bowl, toss in the butter, and cut it in until the mixture resembles bread crumbs. Stir in the sugar and enough water to bind to a dough. Cover and chill 30 minutes.

On a lightly floured surface, roll out the pastry dough and use it to line a 10-inch fluted round flan dish or a 13- x 5-inch rectangular loose-bottomed tart pan. Press the dough well into the dish or pan. Prick the bottom of the pastry case and chill it

BIJANE

Bread with Fruit and Wine

Bijane (you might also come across miot, chicolle, chicolte, or rôtie) is one of several variations found in Touraine as well as Anjou on the theme of fruit in wine with bread, traditionally eaten as a *casse-croûte* at about four o'clock in the afternoon – an alcoholic afternoon tea!

The practice of adding bread to wine was started in the days before the fining of wines (which removes the fine particles of sediment) became so efficient, the bread serving to clarify the wine. *Bijane* is nowadays served as a dessert.

SERVES 4
2 pints ripe strawberries, hulled
about ½ cup vanilla-flavored sugar
about 2½ cups red wine
4 slices of brioche, to serve, toasted if liked

Sprinkle sugar to taste over the strawberries. Pour on the wine, cover with a plate, and leave in a cool place 12 hours. Serve in cold dishes, accompanied by slices of brioche to eat separately or to dunk or crumble into the wine.

LA MOUSSE DE COINTREAU, SAUCE AU MIEL

Cointreau Mousse with Honey Sauce
(Illustrated above right)

For his *gelée d'orange*, Paul Le Quéré of Pavillon Paul Le Quéré (see page 117) makes a syrup of ½ cup of sugar and 6 tablespoons of water, to which he adds 1½ teaspoons unflavored gelatin dissolved in ½ cup of orange juice.

SERVES 6
FOR THE CUSTARD SAUCE
1 vanilla bean
1 cup milk
3 egg yolks
4½ tbsp superfine sugar
FOR THE MOUSSE
grated zest of 1 orange, blanched and well drained
1 envelope unflavored gelatin, dissolved in 3 tbsp water
¼ cup Cointreau
1¼ cups crème fraîche, whipped to soft peaks
flavorless oil, for greasing rings
gelée d'orange (see left)
⅓ cup flower honey
5 tbsp unsalted butter, chopped
red fruits, fresh mint leaves, and saffron threads, to decorate

Add the vanilla bean to the milk and bring gently to a simmer. Cover, remove from the heat, and leave for about 20 minutes.

Strain the milk and use to make a custard sauce with the egg yolks and sugar. Let cool. Add the Cointreau and orange zest to the custard sauce, then stir in the gelatin. Leave until beginning to set, then fold in the whipped cream.

Lightly oil six 3-inch-diameter flan rings and place in the center of 6 cold plates. Divide the orange mixture among them. Chill 2 hours.

Spoon the cooled *gelée d'orange* over the tops and return to the refrigerator to chill 15 minutes longer. Gently melt the honey with the butter, then beat well with an electric mixer. Remove the rings from the mousses, surround them with the honey sauce, and decorate with the red fruit, mint leaves, and saffron.

POIRIER

Pear Cake

A yeast dough is traditional for *poirier* (around Saumur it may be a brioche dough rather than the one given here). It can be finished after cooking by brushing with a glaze made by boiling down the syrup in which the pears were poached, boosted perhaps with *eau-de-vie de poires Williams* or Cointreau.

SERVES 4
1½ cups white bread flour
pinch of salt
7 tbsp vanilla-flavored sugar
½ tbsp quick-rise yeast
2 eggs
6 tbsp milk
4 tbsp unsalted butter, softened plus more
for greasing pan
2-3 ripe pears
½ cup sugar
oil, for greasing bowl

Sift the flour and salt into a bowl, stir in the vanilla-flavored sugar and yeast, and make a well in the center. Beat together the eggs and milk and pour into the well, then stir all the ingredients together until evenly blended and the mixture forms a dough.

Turn onto a lightly floured surface and knead until smooth and elastic. Place in a lightly-oiled bowl, cover with a damp cloth, and let rise until the dough has doubled in volume.

Turn onto the floured surface again and punch down, then lightly knead in the butter. Form into a 5½-inch-diameter round and place in a well-buttered 6-inch round cake pan. Cover with a damp cloth and let rise again.

Meanwhile, peel and core the pears. Over low heat, dissolve the sugar in 2 cups of water, then bring just to a simmer. Add the pears and poach until just tender; the time will vary according to the ripeness of the fruit. Using a slotted spoon, lift the pears from the syrup and slice them evenly.

Preheat the oven to 375°F. Bake the cake about 15 minutes. At the end of this time, take it out and arrange the pears on top. Brush with some of the syrup and return to the oven to bake 15-20 minutes longer, or until the cake is lightly browned. It will be ready when a fine skewer inserted in the center comes out clean.

Serve warm with crème fraîche.

(Left)
Traditional and well-used utensils hang in a busy restaurant kitchen.

CRÉMET D'ANGERS

Cream Cheese Dessert
(Illustrated right)

The prettiest way to serve *crémet d'Angers* is in individual portions using the heart-shaped *cœur à la crème* molds that you can buy in specialty food stores or department stores; or you can make a large quantity in a cheesecloth-lined strainer, and spoon it generously into individual bowls. In Gratien & Meyer's private dining room in Saumur (see page 107), where our example was photographed, they serve this dessert admirably simply, just with fresh strawberries, but the fruit can be currants, nectarines, peaches, apricots, or raspberries.

SERVES 6
2 cups crème fraîche
3-4 egg whites, stifly beaten
plain or vanilla-flavored sugar, fresh fruit (see
above), and crème fraîche, to serve

Line a 3½-cup mold, or 6 individual *cœur à la crème* molds, or a strainer, with cheesecloth.

Whip two-thirds of the crème fraîche until it forms soft peaks. Beat in the egg whites until the mixture is stiff again.

Spoon into the mold(s) or strainer, and leave in a cold place or the refrigerator to drain 8-24 hours (the longer the mixture is left, the firmer it becomes).

Unmold the *crémet(s)* onto a cold plate or plates. Serve with plain or vanilla-flavored sugar, fresh fruit, and crème fraîche.

TO THE SEA

FROM THE VICINITY OF CHAMPTOCEAUX, ON ITS SOUTH BANK, THE LOIRE LEAVES ANJOU AND STARTS THE LAST LEG OF ITS JOURNEY, THROUGH THE PAYS Nantais to the sea. The hills on either side of the river dwindle away in the south, but continue a little further downstream on the opposite shore to Mauves. The banks of the river are mainly reed-fringed, and the land a low, flat, marshy plain of alluvium, changing from mainly pasture to market gardens on the approaches to Nantes. After Nantes, the river passes by an appealingly lonely, low plateau of rough pasture, vineyards, heaths, fen, and little woods. Around Paimbœuf, waters that had a few miles earlier constituted the glorious *fleuve royal*, dissipate into oblivion and become no more than a few drops in the mass of the Atlantic Ocean.

The Atlantic is the major climatic influence here, resulting in pleasant, temperate weather, ideal for growing fruits, early vegetables, and vines. However, the ocean also causes a gentle

(Opposite) The smallholding was at one time the norm for produce grown in the regions of the Pays Nantais, as here near Champtoceaux; but now larger-scale, more commercially viable, market gardens are taking over.
(Above) A Nantais mailbox.

west wind and temperatures can vary wildly, allowing oleanders and umbrella pines to grow to the south of the Loire, but producing damaging frosts well into April.

The Pays Nantais is an administrative creation. It does not have a unified and distinct overall cuisine, because it is made up principally of three very different areas which were only recently brought together under the one name. It is, however, the home of two of the Loire's most famous products, the sauce *beurre blanc* (see pages 131 and 136) and Muscadet wine.

The food in the north and west reflects that of Brittany, while in the east there are Angevin influences. To the south, the coast and the Vendée put their stamp on the cooking. At the heart, in sophisticated, cosmopolitan Nantes, dishes from all three areas exist alongside those owing their origins to its position as a port. From the eighteenth century, sugar, rum, spices, nuts, bananas, and other fruits passed through the city, and inevitably found their way into the cooking. To supply provisions for the crews of the merchant ships, food-processing industries also grew up. The French inventor Nicolas Appert developed the canning process which enabled local fruits and vegetables to be preserved for long sea voyages; fish was also canned. There is still some food manufacturing in Nantes, but of greater gastronomic importance is France's second-largest fresh food wholesale market after Paris's Rungis, which owes its existence to the abundance and caliber of local produce, and good transport links.

Nantais poultry, such as duck, chicken, quail, and guinea fowl, is not actually bred in Nantes. The name is a synonym for the better known and highly-prized Challans poultry. Challans is the town where the birds are reared according to an especially-designated free-range regime (Challans is not the name of a breed), but Nantes was the point from where they were dispatched to the rest of the country, so the packing cases and paperwork were stamped with its name. *Poulets d'Ancenis*, which come from the small town on the northern bank of the Loire almost on the Anjou border, also have a standing locally.

To the south of Nantes, the mild climate, varied soil, and ready access to profitable markets have spawned innumerable market gardens specializing in *primeurs*. The vegetables are mainly those traditionally associated with the area, such as carrots (there is a variety of carrot called "Nantes"), turnips, red radishes, leeks, and potatoes, as well as artichokes and asparagus. It is also the modern center for the growing of the many types of salad leaves that have enjoyed such popularity in recent years: *frisée* (curly endive), two varieties of *mâche* (lamb's lettuce), and commercially grown *pissenlits* (dandelion leaves). Herbs, tomatoes, and strawberries complete the line-up of the major market-garden produce.

For years, the marshes, ponds, and streams of the Marais have provided wild food. Shiny green strands of *salicorne* (salicornia or samphire) are picked early in the spring, before their central spikes form. They are cooked very simply, and eaten like *haricots verts* with butter, perhaps as an accompaniment to oysters, mussels, or salmon. Alternatively, they may be pickled in white wine vinegar, like *cornichons*. If they are not picked until later in the summer, the flesh has to be stripped off the spike by pulling it between the teeth.

1 Mussels and oysters on sale on the Atlantic coast near La Baule. Mussels make the best accompaniment to a typical Muscadet. **2** A selection of rye breads: Rye was the common grain of Brittany, and is still used to make the delicious breads that go well with the region's shellfish. **3** A worker packing celery on a farm outside Nantes. The city has France's second largest wholesale market, and is used particularly for its vegetables. **4** An architectural detail at La Cigale, a seafood restaurant in the center of Nantes noted for its interior. **5** Ivy and ornamental vines on a wall near Champtoceaux. **6** LU is the now very large company that was first created for the production of the original petits beurres cookies. **7** Berlingots are hard candies, variously flavored and colored, and common in the region. **8** Langoustines, minutes away from their watery home, plump and fine-flavored and ready for the pot. **9** At a simple sign like this, the wine will most likely also be simple, although you may be lucky and find a real vinous bargain.

1	2	3
4	5	6
7	8	9

(Above left)
SELECTION OF SEAFOOD
In the Pays Nantais, seafood more or less takes over from freshwater fish; and as there are plenty of customers, especially restaurants, who are willing to pay high prices for good fish, there are plenty of fishermen making a living off the shores.

(Above right)
THE LOIRE
The river peacefully nearing its journey's end.

At one time, another wild food provided in abundance by the marshes were frogs. Although today there is still a limited amount of frog farming, gone are the days when *cuisses de grenouilles* could be seen in fishmerchants, hanging in pairs suspended from wooden skewers. Most of the frogs' legs used in the area now have been imported from eastern Europe, and are usually frozen stiff, although some restaurants buy in live whole frogs. The classic way of serving the legs is with *sauce poulette*, a rich, mild-tasting, pale sauce. Chef Delphin at La Châtaigneraie (see page 146) claims to be one of the only two people surviving who know the true recipe. South of Nantes, a more local accompaniment is a sauce made from the watercress that thrives on the Marais.

Further south, in the Vendée, life has been – and still is – more rural. For instance, Vendéens are fond of beans, especially the variety known as *mojettes* or *mougettes* (see page 138), so called because they are flat and white, with a black line around them, resembling a nun at prayer. *Mojettes* have such a following that a "Confrérie de Mojettes" was formed in the mid-1980s to generate publicity and promote the beans. In the late summer, *mojettes* are eaten fresh, but they are mainly dried for use later in the year in warming *pots au feu*, often in combination with another great standby of the area, cabbage. This occupied such an important place in the local diet that the Royalist insurgents of the Vendée, and later the counter revolutionaries of the 1790s, were dubbed "*Chouans.*"

Vendéen ham is traditionally heavily salted and often eaten raw. Light cooking in butter intensifies the saltiness, and the local means of combating this is to eat it with *mojettes*. Modern, less salty hams can be quite delicious, making a better marriage with ripe (locally grown, of course) charentais melon even than Parma ham.

Cattle were introduced after phylloxera decimated the vineyards in the 1870s. However, trade for the once-important cattle market at Cholet has declined. The local sheep are highly commended by chefs, and in spring there are some *pré-salé* lambs from the coast.

On the other side of the Loire, culture and food take on an altogether different feel and flavor – that of neighboring Brittany. The most obvious evidence of the Breton presence are *galettes* (see page 147). At one time these were used as bread, being dipped into soup, used to mop up juices from a stew, or wrapped around a filling to make a meal in themselves. The custom grew for *galettiers* to sell their wares from stalls, especially along the estuary. In a few places on market days, *galettiers* may still be seen deftly flipping over *galettes* with a wooden *rabot*, before adding an appetizing filling – sweet or savory – as ordered by a waiting customer.

The taste of salt characterizes the cooking of the Pays Nantais, principally because the butter most usually used in cooking is salted. This probably stems from the days when the butter had to be preserved by the addition of salt to slow down the onset of rancidity during long sea voyages, coupled with the occurrence along the Breton coast of natural evaporating pans, *œillets*, for supplying salt from the sea. The first salt of the year, *fleur de sel*, is particularly fine, with a subtle taste other than just that of salt.

There are also plenty of good buttery things to be found in the region. *Pains Nantais* are butter-and-almond cookies biscuits and Nantes is the birthplace of famed "Petit Beurre" cookies, although their originator, Monsieur Lefèvre, did not come from the area. He adapted a recipe which he had brought with him, and the rectangular-shaped cookie grew in popularity, eventually becoming known as "le *Véritable Petit Beurre*." In 1987, a large purpose-built factory was opened just outside Nantes, and now each year 15 million "le Petit Beurre Nantais" come off its production lines.

The buttery sauce you will come across time and time again near the Loire, and in Nantes, is *beurre blanc* (see right). *Beurre blanc* was described by Curnonsky (see page 105) as a "sauce of exquisite finesse and lightness." The shallots which give a discreet seasoning "must be, so to speak, volatized in the vinegar," and should be no more than a remote presence, so must therefore be chopped very finely. Another "secret", according to locals, is to use *demi-sel* (lightly salted) butter. The inclusion of cream, however, is definitely not authentic.

Both Nantais and Angevins claim with quiet certainty that their region is the home of *beurre blanc*. However, it would be wrong to say there is a battle between the two regions over the subject, because each seems oblivious to the claims of the other. In support of their claim, Angevins say that their local shallots have to be used to obtain the necessary subtlety of flavor. I have even been told by an Angevin that *beurre blanc* made in Nantes is not true

BEURRE BLANC
Nantais claim that beurre blanc was "created" – albeit unintentionally – by Madame Clémence, cook to the Marquis de Goulaine at the turn of the

century, during the preparation of a meal for a particularly important dinner party.
With so much to do, she asked one of her assistants to make the sauce béarnaise, while she attended to other things. As the meal was being served, Madame Clémence noticed that something was amiss with the béarnaise – the egg yolks had been omitted! The faulty sauce tasted surprisingly good, which was fortunate because there was no time to replace it, so it was duly served. After the meal, Madame Clémence was summoned to the dining room. Up she went in trepidation, expecting a reprimand, but instead she was congratulated on the "new sauce," and eventually buerre blanc became a classic.

beurre blanc, but beurre Nantais, the shallots having been strained out. Nantais, on the other hand, claim that the sauce originated with a failed *sauce béarnaise* made by one Madame Clémence; her new sauce was such a success that she became a local personality, eventually opening her own restaurant. As so often happens, the sauce is more than likely to have been created in both regions, as both Nantais and Angevin cooks had access to the same ingredients, and because a buttery, slightly sharp sauce is the obvious accompaniment to the dryish, fairly bland river fish that it classically accompanies.

There are some small producers of goat cheese, but the best-known cheese is Curé-Nantais, created in the last century by a priest in an effort to provide food for the poor. Curé-Nantais, resembling St-Paulin both in appearance and flavor, is a flat disk with a golden rind and a paste that is pale straw-colored, smooth, and punctured by small holes. Production of this subtle, rounded, and distinctively flavored cheese is now limited, but look for the cheese from a small farm near Pornic.

Although there is some freshwater fish in the cooking of the Pays Nantais, with the proximity of the estuary and the coast, the fruits of the sea are more in evidence. There is a wealth of sea fish, such as line-caught turbot from the inshore waters of the Atlantic, and seafood, such as scallops, lobsters, a variety of crabs, langoustines, and oysters from the lower stretches of the river and along the estuary. Mussels usually come from further south along the Vendée coast. There is an increasing amount of fish farming, but small fishing ports are still the home of small-scale fishermen. The town of Paimbœuf – which I think acts as a marker for the demise of the Loire – is, for example, a thriving little place, despite the road being partly silted up. The tiny harbor, complete with lighthouse, is busy with boats chugging about laying or hauling in their nets and traps, or unloading eels, enormous lampreys, mullet, and shad by the netful, while their owners bargain on the quayside. Tall reeds rustle at the water's edge, and cafés and bars line the waterfront, while oil-tankers head up-river from the huge refineries at Donges on the opposite shore.

At the dead of a very dark night, or in the early morning from the end of February to early April, when the spring flood-tide washes up the estuary, if you happen to look out across the river near the estuary and see lights bobbing eerily on the water, it will be a flotilla of barges and small boats, each lit with a single lantern. From the boats will be suspended buckets or large carboy-like containers of thick glass attached to cords, in the eager expectation of catching a haul of wriggling, transparent *piballes* or *civelles* (elvers). These immature eels may look as fragile as glass rods, but they will have swum over 2,000 miles from the Sargasso Sea. Provided they elude the buckets and other traps, they will force their way up the Loire until they reach the streams. Here they will stay for up to nine years, to grow into full-size eels, before returning along the river – again having to dodge the hopeful efforts of fishermen to stop them – back to the Atlantic and across to the Sargasso Sea to spawn and die. The favorite local way with *piballes* is to fry them briefly in hot oil until they turn white, then to serve them sizzling hot with salt and pepper.

MARQUIS DE GOULAINE
The family of Robert, Marquis de Goulaine has lived in the same château for 1,000 years. Today the vineyards are large by Muscadet standards and are divided into two distinct areas — the Château de Goulaine with nearby Clos de Montys, and Château de la Grange.

Both Muscadet and Gros Plant are produced, with most of the wines being bottled *sur lie*. Made by traditional vinification methods combined with modern scientific knowledge and meticulous attention to detail, Marquis de Goulaine's Muscadet can be worthy of consideration as a "serious" full-bodied wine.

(Opposite)
GEESE FARMING
The rearing of geese is not traditional in the Loire regions, so this sight of a flock of farmed geese is a rare one. Duck are more commonly bred for the lucrative foie gras and other related products.

(Below)
NEWLY PLANTED VINES
While an older generation turns to more reliable crops, a band of eager younger vignerons is keen to embrace the vine. Newly-planted vines need protecting from the attention of rabbits.

(Below right)
WINE TASTING
Most cost-effective for a small farmer-vigneron is to sell his production direct to the public; driving through the region you will often see simple, handmade signs inviting you for a roadside dégustation (tasting).

WINES

By far the most important wines of the Pays Nantais are Muscadet and Gros Plant, with the former being about treble the latter in volume produced. Muscadet is not a region, but a grape variety that was introduced in the mid-eighteenth century. Before that, most of the wines were red. In 1709, a frost so severe that the coastal waters froze destroyed the existing vines. A move toward white-wine production had already started, so the vines chosen for replanting were of a white variety and included the melon de Bourgogne. In its new home it came to be known as "*muscadet*," literally "small musky one."

There are three Muscadet *appellations*: simple, regional Muscadet, which can come from the largest area but which accounts for only about 10 percent of the output, then slightly better but scarcer (about 5 percent) Muscadet des Coteaux de Loire, and lastly the most severely delimited – and most expensive – Muscadet de Sèvre-et-Maine.

About 85 percent of the Muscadet vineyards lie southeast of Nantes, where the climate is so mild that oleanders and fig trees flourish. The vine has characteristic rounded leaves

and the grapes ripen early, making them susceptible to late frosts, as was the case at the end of April, 1991, when nearly all of the flowers were destroyed in some places. The *vendange* is correspondingly early, usually in September, or even as early as August.

The light structure, restrained alcohol, and naturally low acidity of Muscadet make it liable to oxidation. To keep it fresh, it is bottled by the method unique to the Pays Nantais, known as *sur lie*. When fermentation has stopped, the wine is not transferred to other vats or wooden *fûts*, which could allow contact with air, but instead is left to rest on its lees (sediment) during the following winter, and bottled without racking before June 30 (racking could also give exposure to air and destroy the slight "prickle" of natural carbon dioxide that makes Muscadet tingle pleasantly on the tongue). This system extracts the maximum flavor from the grapes, adding character to the wine. Unfortunately, as it can be a tricky process to carry out well, it also adds to the price.

Muscadet is always dry and light in flavor and alcohol (uniquely, the maximum level, 12 degrees, is laid down in the *appellation* – although this may be increased in exceptional years). Well-made Muscadet is crisp and clean, an easy quaffing wine which needs chilling, making pleasant summer drinking on its own or with mussels or oysters. Poorly made wines, however, are thin and acidic. Top wines of good years can last up to five years, or even 10, but although delicious, they will not taste quite like normal Muscadet.

As in the other Loire regions, the Pays Nantais is an area mainly of small growers, and much of the vinification – as well as about 50 percent of the marketing and selling – is done by the numerous *négociants*. Muscadet began to "take off" in Britain after the Second World War, and by the late 1980s its combination of easy drinking and low price (and familiarity) made it the top-selling white wine in the UK. Either through a desire to "progress" and try out new techniques, or because of concern about the number of vastly improved cheap wines being made further south in France, Spain, and Italy, some growers have been experimenting with *macération pelliculaire* (a process which leaves the fermenting juice in contact with the skins for longer, so more aromatic compounds are extracted – but at the risk of harmful oxidation and excessive acidity), and aging the young wine in new oak barrels. Both of these techniques change the essential *typicité* of Muscadet, and are frowned upon by Muscadet lovers – *vignerons* and drinkers alike.

The "second" wine of the Pays Nantais is Gros Plant. It can be made more or less anywhere in the region and only warrants VDQS status; it, too, can be bottled *sur lie*. Gros Plant is made from the folle blanche, a large greenish grape that produces a simple, light, and dry, sometimes rather acidic, wine.

The area around the small town of Ancenis, on the north bank of the Loire, also produces a small amount of wine, the majority of which (90 percent) is red. Light, smooth, fruity, and slightly aromatic, Coteaux d'Ancenis red wines are best when young and served lightly chilled. The grapes can be gamay à jus blanc, cabernet franc, and cabernet sauvignon. The rosés are lightly fruity, the whites fresh and dry.

LOUIS MÉTAIREAU

Louis Métaireau runs what is often regarded as the most prestigious Muscadet wine business, yet he started with just 4 acres of vines. The driving force responsible for his success, apart from his dynamic personality, is his passionate belief in the *typicité* of Muscadet, and its quality.

In 1957 he formed a group, unique in France, of nine Muscadet *vignerons* who together agree to cooperate in the marketing of their wines. Each grower joins with the others to select their joint fourteen best *cuvées*. At three blind tastings

throughout the year, they eliminate any wines that do not reach a pass mark, and the chosen wines are sold under the Métaireau label. Apart from the kudos of coming first among peers, there is the incentive of 40,000 francs for the producer of the top wine.

JARDINS DE LA FORGE *
1 bis place Piliers
Champtoceaux
Tel 40 83 56 23
See recipe far right

People who have known of this one-time forge for a while will know it as Auberge de la Forge, but when chef-proprietor Paul Pauvert added a *pâtisserie* for the sale of his excellent cakes and pastries, and set aside a small area where they could be enjoyed in *situ* with cups of coffee or tea, he had to change the name as he had changed the restaurant's status. Set on an unusually high spot overlooking the Loire as it begins its final run to the sea, Champtoceaux

commands a wonderful panoramic view of the river. And it seems most appropriate that you can be assured of dining well on dishes made from the best of the particular season's fish from river and sea.

BEURRE BLANC

White Butter Sauce

From Nantes to Orléans, nearly every chef and cook to whom I have spoken has their own version of *beurre blanc*. The most frequent variable is the liquid that is used. Some use all white wine vinegar (which tends to make the sauce rather sharp), some specify that the vinegar should derive from Muscadet wine, and others use a combination of wine and vinegar. Mme Métaireau, wife of the Muscadet *vigneron* (see page 135), uses a bottle of Muscadet for 4 people, which does produce the most well-balanced sauce and is the one I use for special occasions. At other times I use as much Muscadet as I feel fit and add just a touch of white *vinaigre d'Orléans*. (See also page 131.)

SERVES 4

2 shallots, preferably gray, very finely chopped
about ¾ cup Muscadet (see above)
1 tbsp or more white vinaigre d'Orléans
1½ sticks very cold lightly salted butter, diced
salt and freshly ground white pepper

In a small, heavy-bottomed, non-aluminum pan over fairly low heat, simmer the shallots in the wine and vinegar until the shallots have almost dissolved and there is hardly any liquid left.

Remove the pan from the heat and let cool about 30 seconds, then return it to very low heat. Using a small balloon whisk, whisk in the butter one piece at a time, making sure each piece is incorporated before adding the next, to give a smooth sauce with the consistency of thick whipped cream. It should not be too firm, but have distinct body. If at any time the sauce seems to be becoming too warm,

with the butter showing signs of melting, remove the pan from the heat to cool down, but keep whisking.

As the last piece of butter disappears into the sauce, remove the pan from the heat and whisk a few more seconds. Season to taste.

Serve as soon as possible, either with the food it is to accompany, or in a gravy boat warmed to the same temperature as the sauce (which should be only warm, not hot). The sauce can be kept warm for a few minutes before serving by placing the saucepan in a pan of warm water.

SOUPE DE CRUSTACÉS GLACÉE AUX COQUILLAGES

Cold Mixed Seafood Soup

(Illustrated right)

When Paul Pauvert of Les Jardins de la Forge (see left) makes his wonderfully clear-flavored soup, he adds 3½ ounces of lobster shells with the langoustine shells. This does give a better flavor, but as it is neither absolutely necessary nor very realistic for most domestic cooks, I have not included them in this recipe.

SERVES 4-6

20 live langoustines or large raw shrimps
2lb fish bones, preferably from fish such as turbot,
sole, and red mullet
3 onions, chopped
2 slim young leeks, sliced
2 cups Muscadet wine
a fresh bouquet garni consisting of sprigs of parsley,
celery leaves, fennel leaves, thyme, and a bay leaf
20 mussels, 20 cockles, and 40 clams
salt and freshly ground white pepper
chopped fresh basil, chopped parsley, and parsley
sprigs, for garnish

Drop the langoustines or shrimps into boiling water and cook 4-7 minutes until the shells turn red. Drain and let cool before removing the shells and deveining. Reserve the langoustines or shrimps and 4 ounces of the shells.

In a large, heavy-bottomed pot, sweat the fish bones, onions, leeks, and reserved lang-oustine or shrimp shells without any fat or liquid for 4-5 minutes, shaking the pot occasionally to move them around. Stir in the wine, then boil until well reduced. Add 2 cups water and the bouquet garni. Bring to a boil, skim the surface to remove any scum, and then simmer 20-30 minutes, skimming frequently.

Meanwhile, separately steam the mussels, cockles, and clams in covered pans containing a little boiling water about 5-7 minutes until the shells open. Drain well, remove them from their shells, and cool.

Strain the soup through a strainer lined with cheesecloth. Let cool, then season with salt and white pepper. Chill lightly.

Divide all the shellfish among 4 or 6 cold soup plates, scatter the herbs on top and then carefully ladle in the soup. Drink a good Muscadet de Sèvre-et-Maine *sur lie* with this.

MOJETTES SUR CANAPÉS

Vendéen Beans on Toast

Mojettes are softer than many dried beans when cooked, so it is not surprising that they gave rise to this recipe, recalled by Mme Thai-Thuc of an old Vendéen family. In the absence of *mojettes*, try the recipe with well-cooked Lima beans, but do use a good salted butter.

MAKES 1 SLICE
thinnish slice of pain de campagne
salted butter
about 2 spoonfuls of mojettes, cooked until tender

Bake the bread in the oven until just becoming crisp, or toast it slowly. Spread with butter followed by the beans, squashing them as you do so.

For *mojettes au beurre blanc* simply spoon *beurre blanc* (page 136) over the cooked beans.

(Below)
The humble cabbage is a favorite vegetable all along the Loire.

LANGOUSTINES POÊLÉES EN SALADE

Langoustine and Spinach Salad
(Illustrated opposite)

I was discussing with Louis Métaireau (see page 135) how he matched his wines with food. When it came to the cuvée *Cadre Noir*, he said it was perfect with langoustines, especially warm langoustines. A *salade tiède* perhaps? But no, because the acidity of the vinaigrette is an enemy of wine. I put forward the idea of using Muscadet in place of vinegar, as it has a high acidity. Not really, the alcohol would be wrong, and wine would be too diluted. The solution: Boil the wine to drive off the alcohol and concentrate the flavor. Christian Thomas-Trophime, *chef-patron* of La Manoir de la Comète in the southern outskirts of Nantes, was telephoned, and this is the recipe he produced for our lunch; its full title is *Langoustines poêlées et jeunes pousses d'épinards en salade à la réduction d'échalotes au Muscadet*. With it we drank Louis Métaireau's L.M. 1989.

SERVES 4
about 3½-4lb live langoustines or large raw shrimp
2½ cups Muscadet wine
¼ cup finely chopped shallots, preferably gray
salt and freshly ground black pepper
4 small bunches of young spinach leaves
1 tbsp olive oil

Cook the langoustines or shrimp in well-salted boiling water about 3-4 minutes. Drain and let cool completely before removing their shells and deveining.

Boil the Muscadet until it has reduced by three-quarters, then add the shallots and seasoning. Keep warm on the side of the stove, or over very low heat, using a heat diffuser if necessary.

Arrange the spinach leaves on 4 plates. Briefly sauté the shelled langoustines or shrimp with the olive oil, season, and place on the spinach. Pour the Muscadet dressing over the top and serve warm.

CHOUÉE

Cabbage with Butter

The essential elements of this apparently simple dish are the taste of fresh, lightly cooked cabbage, fresh butter, and, most important, the melting of the butter in the heat of the cabbage, not of the stove. Some people add a drop or so of a local white wine vinegar when the cabbage is served; I find that lemon juice makes a good alternative.

Dartrée de choux verts is just another name for what seems to be the same dish, but versions of *chouée* that fricassee the cabbage in butter until it is soft are different altogether.

SERVES 4
4 small heads of green piochon or piochou cabbage or 4 small cabbage hearts, halved
salt and freshly ground black pepper
1 stick fresh salted butter, diced
mild white wine vinegar or lemon juice (optional)

Cook the cabbage in boiling salted water until tender, then drain well. The cabbage may be turned into a serving dish immediately, or mashed and then reheated.

Sprinkle the cabbage with seasoning and add the butter.

Trickle on mild white wine vinegar or lemon juice, if liked, then serve.

ESTOUFFADE DE TURBOT
AU MUSCADET

Turbot with Loire Vegetables and Muscadet

A prize-winners recipe from M. Delphin of La Châtaigneraie (see page 146).

SERVES 4
4 young carrots, cut into cubes
7 tbsp unsalted butter
2 shallots, finely chopped
2 young leeks, finely chopped
4 turbot fillets, cut across into slices
½ bottle of Muscadet wine
⅔ cup crème fraîche
salt and freshly ground pepper
white grapes, seeded, peeled, and warmed in butter
lightly cooked asparagus spears, tossed in butter

Blanch the carrots in boiling salted water 5 minutes. Drain well.

In a Dutch oven, melt 4 tablespoons of the butter, add the shallots, leeks, and carrots, and cook until softened.

Place the turbot on top, pour in wine to come part of the way up, and poach 5 minutes. Take out the fish and vegetables and keep warm. Add any remaining wine to the cooking juices and boil until almost all evaporated. Stir in the crème fraîche and simmer until thick. Remove from the heat and whisk in the remaining butter. Season. Arrange the turbot, vegetables, grapes, and asparagus on 4 warmed plates and pour on the sauce.

(Below)
Turbot as cooked for us at La Châtaigneraie, served with red fruits as a garnish.

TURBOT À LA LIGNE
AUX CÈPES

Turbot with Cèpes

Fishermen still go out from the coast to catch turbot by rod and line rather than in a net, because it is known locally how much better the fish will taste, and many will pay a premium for fish caught this way. The distinguished texture and flavor marry beautifully with those of cèpes.

SERVES 4
4lb turbot, filleted
salt and freshly ground black pepper
1 cup crème fraîche
6 tbsp slightly salted butter, diced, plus more for sautéing
6 tbsp unsalted butter, diced
fleur de sel (see page 131) or coarse sea salt, for sprinkling
2¼lb fresh cèpes, thickly sliced
2 tbsp chopped mixed fresh chervil, chives, and savory
juice of 1 lemon

Season the turbot very lightly.

Boil the crème fraîche until reduced by half. Over low heat, gradually whisk in the two butters, one piece at a time, making sure each piece is fully incorporated before adding the next. Keep it warm.

Dry the turbot in a nonstick pan, without any fat, until lightly colored on each side. Sprinkle with *fleur de sel* or sea salt.

Quickly sauté the cèpes in butter until lightly browned (or "given the color of autumn" as the original French recipe states). Add the herbs, seasoning, and lemon juice to taste. Pour the sauce onto 4 warmed plates, place the fish on top, and scatter on the cèpes.

ALOSE GRILLÉE, SAUCE L'OSEILLE

Grilled Shad with Sorrel Sauce

(Illustrated below)

The best shad I have ever eaten was plainly grilled over a fire of grapevine prunings, built on the river bank. Crusty bread and a bottle of Loire Sauvignon completed the feast. (The fish below was photographed at Beau Rivage, see right.)

Normally, however, I follow tradition and serve shad with sorrel, either wrapping the fish in the leaves or making a stuffing or sauce (see page 98).

SERVES 4-6
2lb shad, dressed
salt and freshly ground black pepper

1½ cups dry white Anjou wine
1 shallot, finely chopped
2 sticks unsalted butter, chilled and diced
about 5oz sorrel, torn into shreds (about 2½ cups)

Season the fish inside and out, and then place it over hot charcoal or under a pre-heated broiler about 10 minutes on each side, or until the fish is browned and the flesh flakes easily when tested with the point of a knife.

Meanwhile, simmer the wine and shallot until reduced to about 3 tablespoons. Heat 2 tablespoons of the butter in another pan, add the sorrel and cook, stirring occasionally, until wilted. Lower the heat under the wine and shallots to very low and gradually beat in the remaining butter, making sure each piece is fully incorporated before adding the next. Beat in the sorrel and adjust the seasoning.

BEAU RIVAGE

Clermont-sur-Loire
Le Cellier
Tel 40 25 46 40
See recipe this page

The tiny hamlet of Le Cellier is down a small road off the N23 between Nantes and Angers. The Beau Rivage is at the end of the road, overlooking the Loire, just downstream from Champtoceaux on the opposite bank. The restaurant now belongs to Jacques Grelet and his wife Marie-Christine. Although M. Grelet spent much of his working life as a *pâtissier* in Paris, he now draws more upon the diverse knowledge and experience gained during his childhood at his parents'

restaurant in Orléans, to include all types of dishes – and particularly the classic Loire fish – on his menu.

POULET MARAÎCHER

Chicken with Vegetables

This is a dish for the late spring when colorful *primeurs* from the many *maraîchers* (market gardeners) are at their best.

SERVES 4-6
1 stick unsalted butter
3lb free-range chicken, cut into pieces
8 small carrots
8 small leeks
8 small turnips
salt and freshly ground black pepper
2 tbsp chopped mixed fresh herbs, including
parsley, thyme, chervil, and bay
½ cup good-quality Muscadet wine
⅔ cup chicken stock

Melt half of the butter in a wide, shallow pan. Add the chicken pieces in a single layer and cook gently, uncovered, about 15 minutes, turning them occasionally, until golden. Meanwhile, melt the remaining butter in another pan. Add the vegetables and cook, shaking the pan occasionally, about 8 minutes.

Add the vegetables and cooking juices to the chicken. Season, cover the pan, and cook gently about 30 minutes, until the chicken and vegetables are tender. Sprinkle with the herbs, shake the pan well, and cook for a further 3-4 minutes longer. Transfer the chicken and vegetables to a warmed serving plate and keep warm.

Skim the fat from the cooking juices and stir in the wine, scraping in the sediment. Bring to a boil and reduce to about 2 tablespoons, then add the stock and reduce by about half. Check the seasoning. Serve the sauce in a warmed gravy boat with the chicken and vegetables.

CANARD NANTAIS AU MUSCADET

Duck in Muscadet

This recipe is based on an old family recipe of Mme Métaireau, wife of one of the leading Muscadet *vignerons* (see page 135). The acidity of Muscadet helps to counteract the richness of the duck. Wine grapes should be used when they are available, but during the rest of the year dried currants, not grapes, are substituted as they have a better combination of sweetness and sharpness than dessert grapes.

SERVES 4-5
up to 1 quart good-quality Muscadet wine
1lb veal shank
1lb onions, halved
1lb carrots, halved
a bouquet garni
salt
¾ cup dried currants
6-lb duck, preferably free-range and a special
breed,
such as Lunesdale
1 stick and 2 tbsp unsalted butter, diced

The day before the duck is required, slowly simmer together half of the Muscadet, the veal, onions, carrots, bouquet garni, a pinch of salt, and 2 cups of water for 4 hours. Strain the stock and let cool, then remove the fat from the surface. Soak the currants in a little of the remaining wine.

The next day, preheat the oven to 350°F. Place the duck on a rack in a roasting pan and roast 20 minutes.

Heat the remaining Muscadet in a large Dutch oven, then add the duck and cook, covered, over low heat on top of the stove about 1¼-1½ hours, the time de-

pending on the quality and size of the bird you are cooking.

Drain the currants. Heat the cold stock without allowing it to boil. Using a fork, gradually whisk the butter into it, making sure each piece is fully incorporated before adding the next. When all the butter has been added, add the currants.

Cut the duck into serving portions and place on a hot serving plate. Pour on the sauce and serve at once.

CUL DE LAPIN À LA NANTAISE

Rabbit with Mushrooms and Shallots

SERVES 4
1 young wild rabbit, dressed and cut into pieces
salt and freshly ground black pepper
2¼ cups Muscadet wine
1 small carrot, sliced

3 shallots, preferably gray, finely chopped
2 sprigs of fresh thyme
¼ lb lightly salted sliced bacon, sliced across into strips
½ lb mushrooms, fresh wild one if possible
7 tbsp lightly salted butter, diced
finely chopped parsley, to garnish

Season the rabbit pieces with pepper and a little salt. Put them in a bowl with the wine, carrot, shallots and one of the sprigs of thyme, and let marinate about 24 hours.

Remove the rabbit from the marinade, allowing excess to drain off, and pat dry. Strain the marinade; reserve the liquid and shallots. Cook the bacon strips in a heavy-based saucepan until they begin to color and the fat runs. Remove with a slotted spoon and reserve.

Increase the heat, add the rabbit pieces to the pan, and cook until lightly browned. Remove and reserve. Lower the heat again, add the mushrooms and shallots, and cook gently, shaking the pan occasionally, about 4-5 minutes.

Remove with a slotted spoon and reserve. Add the marinade liquid to the pan. Boil 2-3 minutes. Lower the heat so the liquid is barely simmering, then return the rabbit pieces, half of the mushrooms, the bacon strips and the second sprig of thyme. Cover and cook gently, turning the rabbit pieces occasionally, about 1 hour until tender. Transfer the rabbit to a warmed plate, cover, and keep warm.

Boil the liquid until reduced by half, then lower the heat and gradually swirl in the butter, making sure each piece is fully incorporated before adding the next.

Return the rabbit to the sauce, along with any juices that have collected on the plate, and the shallots and remaining mushrooms. Heat through without boiling. Adjust the seasoning according to taste and sprinkle with the parsley.

(Left)
At Les Maraîchers in Nantes, rabbit pieces are served surrounded by delicious wild mushrooms, with a sauce made from the cooking juices served separately. The recipe given above can be presented in this way simply by not returning the rabbit to the sauce at the end.

PÊCHES DES VIGNES

White Peaches in Wine

One of my most memorable culinary experiences was eating a white peach freshly plucked from the tree, its flesh still warm from the sun. That year had been dry with plenty of sunshine, and the fruit, never very large, was particularly small, and packed with wonderful flavor.

White peach trees (it is the peaches that are white, not the trees) do particularly well in the Pays Nantais climate and were once a common sight in the Muscadet vineyards. They were not planted to act as an early indication of disease, as is the case with roses in Bordeaux, but simply, I was assured by Pierre Luneau of La Grange, because they grow in the same conditions and can be treated in the same way as the vines (and, perhaps most importantly, because the *vignerons* like eating them). Vineyard white peach trees are, sadly, not as common as they once were because they get in the way of modern plows, tractors, and other machinery.

This is how Madame Luneau prepares their *pêches des vignes* for the *vendangeurs*.

SERVES 4
6 ripe pêches des vignes, or white-fleshed peaches
about 3 tbsp superfine sugar, preferably
vanilla-flavored
1½-2 cups white wine, preferably Coteaux du
Layon

Peel the peaches (if really ripe, there should be no need to pour boiling water over the fruit). Cut them in half and remove the pits.

Put the peach halves into a bowl and sprinkle with sugar according to the sweetness of the fruit. Leave until the sugar has dissolved, then pour on enough white wine to cover.

Place a plate on top to keep the peaches submerged and leave overnight in a very cool place, or in the refrigerator. Serve at this temperature.

GALETTES NANTAISES

Nantais Butter Cookies

Rich, buttery *galettes Nantais* are very similar to *galette* or *gâteau bretonne*, except that the dough is cut into small cookies rather than being baked in a large round.

MAKES ABOUT 18
1 stick unsalted butter, softened
½ cup vanilla-flavored sugar
3 egg yolks, beaten
1⅔ cups flour
pinch of salt
egg yolk beaten with cold water, for glazing

Beat the butter and sugar together until soft, then beat in the egg yolks. Gently fold in half of the flour and the salt. When just evenly mixed, fold in the remaining flour. Using a round-bladed knife, lightly form into a dough, then knead just until it no longer sticks to the fingers. Cover and chill. Using a lightly floured rolling pin on a lightly floured surface, roll out the dough thinly. Cut out rounds with a diameter of about 2 inches. Brush with the glaze. Carefully transfer to a baking sheet, taking care not to distort the shapes. Chill about 30 minutes.

Preheat the oven to 375°F. Bake the *galettes* about 10 minutes. Let cool slightly, then carefully transfer to a wire rack to cool.

BOURDAINES

Apples in Pastry
(Illustrated opposite)

Bourdaines is the most common name for this apple dessert, but *bourdanes* or *bambolles* may also be used. Enclose a peeled pear or a peach (not too ripe and soft) instead of the apple for *bourdaines à la poire*, or *pêche* – in which case the cooking time can be reduced by about 20 minutes, depending on the firmness of the fruit.

SERVES 4
1⅔ cups flour
pinch of salt
1 stick unsalted butter, diced
2 tsp sugar
4 large apples, peeled and cored
4 heaping tsp quince or plum preserves
milk, cream, or beaten egg, for glazing

Mix the flour and salt and cut in the butter it until the mixture resembles bread crumbs. Stir in the sugar, then, using a round-bladed knife, lightly bind to a soft but not sticky dough with 2-3 tablespoons of water. Cover and chill 30 minutes.

Preheat the oven to 350°F.

Divide the dough into 4 pieces. On a floured surface, roll out each piece to a square large enough to enclose an apple.

Set an apple in the center of each square and place a teaspoonful of the preserves in each apple cavity. Dampen the edges of the pastry and fold around the apples to make pyramid shapes, sealing the edges together well. Brush lightly with milk, cream, or beaten egg. Place on a buttered baking sheet. Bake about 45 minutes, or until the apples are tender. Cover with foil if the pastry becomes too brown.

LA CHÂTAIGNERAIE **
156 route Carquefou
Sucé-sur-Erdre
Tel 40 77 90 95
See recipes on this page and
page 140

La Châtaigneraie opened in its
idyllic setting, overlooking the
river Erdre and 10 miles from

the center of Nantes, on
November 9, 1988. Joseph
Delphin had already gained a
name for himself at his
restaurant closer to Nantes, after
moving there in 1961. When his
son, Jean-Louis, joined him
there, however, larger premises
were needed to allow them
both to utilize and develop their
individual talents more fully.
Mme Delphin is also actively
involved. The restaurant is now
in a classified manor house,
built in 1872 out of tufa and
situated in beautiful parkland
with its own lake. Full advantage
is taken of the variety and
quality of fish and shellfish from
the river, estuary and coast, as
well as local frogs' legs.

SORBET AU MUSCADET

Muscadet Sorbet

(Illustrated above)

This recipe was supplied to me by Joseph
Delphin of La Châtaigneraie (see left).

SERVES 6-8
1 cup sugar
juice of 1 lemon
1 bottle of Muscadet wine
edible leaves, to decorate
crisp cookies, such as tuile d'amandes, to serve

In a heavy-based saucepan, heat the sugar
in 1 cup of water, stirring until dissolved.
Then bring to a boil and simmer 2 minutes. Let cool.

Strain in the lemon juice and add the
wine.

Chill, then transfer to an ice-cream
maker. Alternatively, pour into a metal
container and place in the freezer. Freeze
until half set and mushy, then turn into a
chilled bowl and beat to break up the ice
crystals. Return to the container and
freeze until firm, repeating the beating
twice more.

Decorate with edible leaves and serve
with crisp cookies.

GALETTES

Buckwheat crêpes

(Illustrated above)

Buckwheat *galettes* are usually served with a savory filling; among the most delicious is grated Cantal or goat cheese.

Buckwheat is sold in some health food stores, but if it is unavailable – or if you intend to use a sweet filling – use all wheat flour. To make richer *galettes*, replace half to three-quarters of the water with milk.

MAKES 6
1 cup and 2 tbsp buckwheat flour
¾ cup all-purpose flour
pinch of salt
¼ cup clarified butter, melted, plus more for greasing pan and serving

Stir the flours and salt together and make a well in the center. Gradually stir in ⅔ cup of water, keeping the mixture smooth, and beat well. Stir in a further ⅔ cup of water and beat well. Still beating, add ⅔ cup or a little more of water to give a batter with the consistency of thick cream. Finally beat in the butter.

Rub a large crêpe pan or heavy skillet with a piece of well-buttered paper and heat until a drop of batter sizzles immediately when it is dropped into it.

Pour 2 or 3 spoonfuls of the batter into the pan, tipping it so the batter coats the bottom evenly. Cook over high heat until the *galette* is set and lightly colored underneath. Turn and cook the other side.

Dot butter over it immediately without allowing it to cook further. Fold in four, add a filling, and serve very hot.

FAR BRETON

Prune Batter Pudding

Traditionally, a *far breton* is made in large rounds and served cut into wedges while still lukewarm. When cold it will be more solid. The mixture can also be cooked in individual ramekin dishes. The cooking of Brittany is a significant influence on that of the Pays Nantais, and you will find many Breton specialties, such as this one, all over the region.

This version has more eggs but less flour than some, so it is richer, lighter, more tender – and quite delicious.

SERVES 4
7oz prunes
¼ cup rum (optional)
2 tbsp unsalted butter
7 tbsp flour
3½ tbsp granulated sugar
4 eggs, beaten
2 cups milk
confectioners' sugar, for dusting

Soak the prunes in the rum or the same quantity of warm water about 2 hours.

Put the butter into a shallow baking dish and place in the oven while heating it to 400°F. Mix the flour and granulated sugar together in a bowl, then gradually stir in the eggs, followed by the milk, stirring constantly to keep the batter smooth. Drain the liquid from the prunes and stir it into the batter.

Put the prunes into the hot butter in the dish. Carefully pour in the batter and bake about 1 hour or until the pudding is well risen, just set in the center, and golden brown on the top. Let cool slightly, then serve warm, dusted with confectioners' sugar.

A VISITOR'S GUIDE

To provide a comprehensive guide to all the restaurants and places of interest in such a wide area is beyond the scope of this book, but listed below is a compilation of various recommendations. It includes a wide range of restaurants where it is felt you will have an enjoyable meal.

All the major towns, as well as many smaller places, have an *office de tourisme* or *syndicat d'initiative*, which will provide current information about local fairs and festivals, and opening times of places of interest; some also have information on restaurants and shops.

Wild mushroom gathering, shooting, and fishing may appear to be ubiquitous, but beware. Stay off private land and keep a watchful eye open for signs stating *chasse privé* or *champignons interdit*, which expressly forbid hunting and mushrooming. There are closed seasons for game, but they are not always the same everywhere along the Loire, so check at the local town hall or police station. There are also seasons governing fishing which apply to particular stretches of water (classified as Category A or Category B). Detailed advice can be obtained from a local fishing tackle shop, which will also often sell permits. Fishing permits are issued for use within a *département*, and are valid for a year.

If you gather wild mushrooms, only pick those you are certain are safe and if you are in any doubt at all, check them against the color charts displayed at drugstores; the pharmacist will also identify species for you. PLEASE NOTE THAT WHILE EVERY EFFORT HAS BEEN MADE TO PROVIDE ACCURATE INFORMATION, ALL ADDRESSESS, TELEPHONE NUMBERS, AND OPENING TIMES ARE LIABLE TO CHANGE.

VINEYARD VISITING

In the wine-producing areas, there are many signs indicating wine tastings (*dégustations*) and visits, so unless you are particularly interested in specific wines it is not necessary to make any arrangements beforehand. However, remember that most will close between noon and 2 p.m. for lunch, and do not expect to be greeted with much enthusiasm if you visit during the *vendange*. Some visits and tastings are free, sometimes a charge is made.

The *maison des vins*, and sometimes the *syndicat d'initiative*, will have up-to-date details of places where visitors are welcome, whether just for a tasting, or for a guided tour, or both, and whether English is spoken. They will also know if an appointment is necessary, and should arrange it.

AUVERGNE, NIVERNAIS AND BOURBONNAIS

Restaurants

LA BRUSCADE
place de la Résistance
Antraigues Tel 75 38 72 92
Closed Wednesday; from June through September closed Tuesday and Wednesday

LO PODELLO
Antraigues Tel 75 38 71 48
Closed October 1 – March 31, June, Thursday

LE PRÉ BOSSU *
Moudeyres
Tel 71 05 10 70
Closed first weekend November
through Easter, Tuesday lunch, and Wednesday off-season

AUBERGE JEAN LE DINDON
Le Bourg
Chaudeyrolles
Tel 71 59 56 82
Closing days not fixed, so best to call ahead

LA MARMITE
61 rue des Lacs
St-Flour Tel 71 60 03 06
Open daily all year

CHEZ GUITOU
Saint-Poncy
Massiac Tel 71 73 11 62
Closed December 21 – 28, January 2 – 21

AUBERGE DU MOULIN DE CIVADOUX
Sauxillanges
Tel 73 96 81 94
Closed January, Tuesday evening, and Wednesday

LE BOUT DU MONDE
Saint-Georges
Tel 71 60 15 84
Closing days not fixed, so best to call ahead

AUBERGE DES CIMES
Saint-Bonnet-le-Froid
Tel 71 59 93 72
Closed November 15 through Easter, Wednesday, Sunday evenings in the off season

MARC ET CHRISTINE
29 avenue Marc-Seguin
Annonay Tel 75 33 46 97
Closed January 2 – 24, Monday (except holidays), Sunday eves

LE PATIO
29 avenue Marc-Seguin
Annonay Tel 75 67 58 41
Closed August

PIERRE GAGNAIRE
7 rue de la Richelandière
Saint-Étienne
Closed Sunday, Monday

AUBERGE DES TERRASSES
Saint-Symphorien-de-Lay
Tel 77 64 72 87
Closed January, 1 week in August, Sunday eves, Monday

LA RENAISSANCE **
N7 Magny-Cours
nr. Nevers Tel 86 58 10 40
Closed late February through late March, August, Sunday evenings, Monday

HÔTEL DU PONT DU CHER
2 avenue de la Gare
Orval Tel 48 96 00 51
Closed Sunday evenings, Monday

LE MOULIN DE CHAMÉRON
route de Sancoins
Bannegon Tel 48 61 83 80
Closed November 15 – March 1, Tuesday off-season

Markets

Le Monastier-sur-
  Gazeille: *Tuesday*
Fay-sur-Lignon: *Wednesday*
Saugues: *Monday, Friday*
Le-Puy-en-Velay:
  Wednesday, Saturday
Siaugues-Saint-Marie:
  Sunday
Langeac: *Tuesday, Thursday*
Tence: *Tuesday*
Le Chambon-sur-Lignon:
  Saturday
Yssingeaux: *Thursday,*
  Saturday
Montfaucon-en-Velay:
  Wednesday
Riotord: *Friday*
Monistrol-sur-Loire: *Friday*
Saint-Didier-en-Velay:
  Wednesday
Annonay: *Wednesday,*
  Saturday
Saint-Genest-Malifaux:
  Thursday, Sunday
Aurec-sur-Loire:
  Wednesday, Friday, Sunday
Firminy: *Tuesday, Thursday*
Saint-Étienne: *daily*
Andrézieux-Bouthéon:
  Tuesday, Thursday, Friday
Montbrison: *Saturday*
Montrond-les-Bains:
  Thursday
Balbigny: *Monday*
Violay: *Tuesday, Sunday*
Roanne: *Tuesday, Friday,*
  Saturday, Sunday
Ambierle: *Thursday*
Marcigny: *Monday*
Lapalisse: *Thursday*
Saint-Pourçain: *Saturday*
Le Donjon: *Tuesday*
Paray-le-Monial: *Friday*

Digoin: *Friday, Sunday*
Bourbon-Lancy: *Saturday*
Decize: *Friday*
Saint-Amand-Montrond:
  Wednesday
Orval: *Friday*
Sancoins: *Wednesday*
Guerche-sur-l'Aubois:
  Tuesday
Nevers: *Saturday*
Guerigny: *Friday*
La Charité-sur-Loire:
  Saturday

Places of interest

CHÂTEAU DU
MONASTIER
Le Monastier-sur-Gazeille
Tel 71 03 80 01
Closed Saturday and Sunday
lunchtimes

FERME DES FRÈRES
PERREL
Moudeyres Tel 71 05 12 13
Closed September 16 – July 7,
lunchtimes

MUSÉE POPULAIRE DU
MASSIF-CENTRAL
Saint-Didier-en-Velay
Tel 71 66 22 61
Closed September 2 – July 1,
mornings

MAISON DE LA BÉATE,
MUSÉE DES ARTS ET
TRADITIONS PAYSANNES
Marlhes
Saint-Genest-Malifaux
Tel 77 51 24 76
Open Sunday afternoons only,
September 16 – July 15

LA JASSERIE DU COQ
NOIR
Col des Supeyres
Saint-Anthème
Tel 73 82 03 11
Closed last Sunday June
through last Sunday September

MAISON SAUVAGNARDE
Sauvain
Saint-Georges-en-Couzan
Tel 77 76 81 83
Closed September 26 – June 5,
Sunday, mornings

MUSÉE ALICE-TAVERNE
Ambierle Tel 77 65 60 99
Closed December 1 –
February 1, lunchtimes

MUSÉE DE CHARROUX
ET DE SON CANTON
rue de la Poulaillerie
Charroux
Chantelle Tel 70 56 85 25
Closed October 1 – June 30,
mornings

MUSÉE DE LA VIGNE
ET DU VIN
Cour des Bénédictins
Saint-Pourçain-sur-Sioule
Tel 70 45 32 73
Closed January – February, and
mornings September 16 – June 14

MUSÉE RURAL DE LA
SOLOGNE
BOURBONNAISE
Mairie de Beaulon
Beaulon
Chevagnes Tel 70 42 70 89
Open Sunday and holiday
afternoons in summer

MUSÉE DU PLAIX
Lignières Tel 48 60 00 18
Open Sunday afternoons in
summer

AU BURON
(*see Cantal being made*)
Salilhes
Thiézac Tel 71 47 52 16
Closed lunchtimes and Sunday
afternoons

SYNDICAT D'INITIATIVE
(*will arrange visits to burons*)
place Tissandier-d'Escous
Salers Tel 71 40 70 68

Specialties of the region

ALAIN COMTE
43 Fixe-St-Geneys
Tel 71 57 02 12

AU NÉGUS
96 rue du Commerce
Nevers Tel 86 61 06 85
Closed Sunday, Monday
mornings, lunchtimes

PÂTISSERIE-CONFISERIE
EDE
75 rue du Commerce
Nevers Tel 86 61 02 97
Closed Sunday afternoons, Mon

Festivals/Fairs

Saugues: (*mid-July*) "Foire aux Bestiaux" Animal Fair
  (*early October*) "Foire aux Champignons" Mushroom Fair
Aiguilhe: (*last weekend in September*) "Foire au Miel" Honey Fair
Yssingeaux: (*late December*) "Marché au Foie Gras Frais de
  Canard" Fresh foie gras market
Saint-Bonnet-le-Froid: (*early November*) "Foire aux Cèpes"
  Wild Mushroom Fair
Annonay: (*early December*) "Rôtie Monstre de Châtaignes"
  Chestnut-Roasting Festival
Sauvain: (*mid-August*) "Fête de Myrtilles" Bilberry Festival
Montbrison: (*early October*) "Journées de la Fourme"
  Montbrison cheese days
Panissières: (*early April*) "Fête du Printemps" Spring Festival
  (*late June*) "Fête de la Saint Jean"
Thiers: (*September 14*) "Foire au Pré" Traditional Fair
  (*December 7*) "Saint-Eloi des Goges" Food Festival
Roanne: (*October 5-10*) "Foire Froide"
Saint-Pourçain-sur-Sioule: (*last weekend in February*) "Foire
  aux Vins"
  (*last weekend in August*) "Foire des Vins"
Bruère-Allichamps: (*end of September*) "Foire aux Fromages"
  Cheese Fair
Clamecy: (*early August*) "Fête de l"Andouille" Chitterling
  Sausage Festival

SOLOGNE AND ORLÉANAIS

Restaurants

AUBERGE ALPHONSE
MELLOT
16 Nouvelle Place
Sancerre Tel 48 54 20 53
*Closed mid-December through
mid-January, Wednesday*

LA TOUR
place Halle
Sancerre Tel 48 54 00 81
*Closed March 4 – 15,
December 16 – January 10,
Monday evenings, Tuesday*

L'ÉTOILE
2 quai de la Loire
Sancerre Tel 48 54 12 15
*Closed mid-November through
February, Wednesday*

RIVAGE *
1 quai Nice
Gien Tel 38 67 20 53
*Closed early February through
early March*

AUBERGE DES
TEMPLIERS **
N7 Les Bézards
Tel 38 31 80 01
*Closed mid-January through
mid-February*

GUILLAUME DE LORRIS
8 Grande Rue
Lorris Tel 38 94 83 55
*Closed Wednesday, Tuesday
evenings*

LE VIEUX RELAIS
2 route d'Isles
Vannes-sur-Cosson
Tel 38 58 04 14
*Closed September 7-15,
December 22 – January 15,
Sunday evenings and Monday
(except June 15 – August 31)*

ROBERT PESSON
54 rue du General de
Gaulle
Meung-sur-Loire
Tel 38 44 75 14
Closed Sunday and Monday

AUBERGE DU CHÂTEAU
Talcy Tel 54 81 03 14
*Closed Monday evenings,
Tuesday*

BERNARD ROBIN **
1 avenue Chambord
Bracieux Tel 54 46 41 22
*Closed December 23 –
January 30, Tuesday evenings,
Wednesday*

HÔTEL SAINT-
HUBERT **
rue Nationale
Cour-Cheverny
Tel 54 79 96 60
*Closed Tuesday evenings and
Wednesday*

GRAND HÔTEL DU
LION D'OR **
69 rue Georges
Clemenceau
Romorantin-Lanthenay
Tel 54 76 00 28
*Closed early January through
mid-February*

MOULIN DE VILLIERS
Nouan-le-Fuzelier
Tel 54 88 72 27
*Closed January through end
March, and first 2 weeks
September. Closed Tuesday and
Wednesday in November and
December*

HÔTEL DE LA PLAGE
42 rue du Pont
Chabris Tel 54 40 02 24
*Closed December 23 – through
early February, Sunday
evenings, Monday off-season*

GRAND HÔTEL ST-
AIGNAN
7 quai Jean Jacques
Delorme
St-Aignan-sur-Cher
Tel 54 75 18 04
*Closed Sunday eves, Monday,
December 15 – February 1*

Markets

Bourges: *Wednesday,
Thursday, Friday, Saturday,
Sunday*
Menetou-Salon: *Sunday*
Sancerre: *Saturday, Tuesday
(March-November)*
Pouilly-sur-Loire: *Friday*
Cosnes-sur-Loire:
Wednesday, Sunday
Aubigny-sur-Nère:
Saturday
Gien: *Wednesday, Saturday*
Lorris: *Thursday*
Montargis: *Wednesday,
Saturday*
Orléans: *Tuesday,
Wednesday, Thursday,
Saturday*

La Ferté-Saint-Aubin:
Thursday
Lamotte-Beuvron: *Friday*
Beaugency: *Saturday*
Vendôme: *Friday, Sunday*
Mer: *Thursday*
Blois: *Tuesday, Wednesday,
Thursday, Saturday, Sunday*
Bracieux: *Thursday*
Contres: *Friday*
Romorantin-Lanthenay:
Wednesday, Saturday
Selles-sur-Cher: *Sunday*
Noyers-sur-Cher: *Sunday*
Montrichard: *Monday,
Friday*

Places of interest

MUSÉE DU BERRY
4 rue des Arénes
Bourges Tel 48 70 41 92
*Closed Tuesday, Sunday
mornings, holidays, lunchtimes*

FAIENCERIE DE GIEN
78 place de la Victoire
Gien Tel 38 67 00 05
Closed holidays

MUSÉE INTERNATIONAL
DE LA CHASSE
place du Château
Gien Tel 38 67 69 69
Closed December and January

MUSÉE DES TANNEURS
Ilot des Tanneurs
1 rue du Château
Montargis Tel 38 95 10 00
*Open Saturday afternoons, first
Sunday every month*

MUSÉE DE L'ARTISANAT
RURAL ANCIEN
Clos Rolland du Roxcoat
Tigy Tel 38 58 00 42
*Open Sunday and holiday
afternoons, Easter, last Sunday
October, Saturday in summer,
every day for groups*

MUSÉE DE LA
TONNELLERIE (cooperage)
La Cour des Muids
1 rue de Patay
Checy Tel 38 62 72 45
*Open Saturday afternoons,
Sunday, Easter, holidays*

DOMAINE DE CIRAN
Le Ciran
Menestreau-en-Villette
La Ferté-Saint-Aubin
Tel 38 76 90 93
Closed Tuesday, lunchtimes

MUSÉE DUNOIS
2 place Dunois
Beaugency Tel 38 44 55 23
Closed Tuesday

MUSÉE DE LA
CORBILLIÈRE
Mer Tel 54 81 10 98
*Open afternoons July and
August*

MUSÉE MUNICIPAL DE
VENDÔME
Cour du Cloître
Vendôme Tel 54 77 26 13
*Closed Tuesday, holidays,
lunchtimes*

CHÂTEAU DE
CHAMBORD
(wild game park)
Chambord Tel 54 20 31 32
Closed holidays

MUSÉE DE SOLOGNE
Hôtel de Ville
1 rue Faubourg-Saint-
Roch
Romorantin
Tel 54 76 07 06
*Closed Tuesday, Sunday
mornings, lunchtimes*

MUSÉE D'HISTOIRE ET
TRADITIONS LOCALES
Cloître de l'Ancienne
Abbaye
Selles-sur-Cher
Tel 54 97 40 19
*Open in summer, Tuesday and
Thursday afternoons, weekends*

LOCATURE DE LA
STRAIZE
Gy-en-Sologne
Tel 54 83 82 89
*Closed mid-November through
end March, lunchtimes,
Tuesday*

MUSÉE DE
L'AGRICULTURE ET DE
LA VITICULTURE
La Presles-d'Oisly
Contres Tel 54 79 52 69
*Open in summer, Tuesday and
Saturday afternoons*

Specialties of the region

Many good artisanal food
shops in and around
Romorantin-Lanthenay
and on the Grand rue and
rue Gambetta in Jargeau.

À LA RENOMÉE
5 mail Ouest
Pithiviers Tel 38 30 00 24

PÂTISSERIE BEAUFORT
23 rue de l'Amiral
Gourdon
Pithiviers Tel 38 30 00 21
*Closed Monday, lunchtimes,
August*

CHOCOLATERIE
ROYALE
(M. Chavanette)
51 rue Royale
Orléans Tel 38 53 93 43
*Closed Sunday, Monday
mornings, lunchtimes*

AUX DÉLICES
(Philippe Berteault)
52 avenue de l'Hôtel-de-
Ville
Lamotte-Beuvron
Tel 54 88 10 08
Closed Monday

HÔTEL TATIN
5 avenue de Vierzon
Lamotte-Beuvron
Tel 54 88 00 03
*Closed last 3 weeks in January,
Sunday evenings, Monday*

ÉTABLISSEMENT
GUENARD
(Huileries du Berry)
ZI du Greletier
42 rue de Tours
Noyers-sur-Cher
Tel 54 75 09 09
*Closed weekends, 2 weeks in
winter, 3 weeks in summer*

LA MAISON DU SAFRAN
21 route des Pativiers
Boyne
Tel 38 33 13 84, 38 33 13 05
Open April 1 – November 11

BERGERIES DE
SOLOGNE (products from
Sologne breed of sheep)
Ferme de Gaugeny
Fontaines-en-Sologne
Tel 54 46 45 61
Open every day

Vineyard Visiting

DOMAINE VACHERON
Caves Saint-Pierre
1 rue de Puits Poulton
Sancerre Tel 48 54 09 93
*Closed end September through
October*

M. GAUMIER
route de Lury-sur-Arnon
Lury-sur-Arnon
Quincy Tel 48 51 31 55
*Open by appointment
Monday – Friday*

L'UNION VITICOLE
SANCERROISE
16 bis avenue Nationale
Sancerre Tel 48 54 03 51

CLAUDE LAFOND
Le Bois St Denis
Reuilly Tel 54 49 22 17
Open by appointment

SYNDICAT VITICOLE
DE POUILLY
Les Loges
Pouilly-sur-Loire
Tel 86 39 12 65

DOMAINE GUY SARGET
route Nationale 7
Pouilly-sur-Loire
Tel 86 39 16 37
*Closed Christmas and
New Year*

Festivals/Fairs

Pouilly-sur-Loire: *(August 15)* "Foire aux Vins"
Menetou-Salon: *(August 15)* "Journée caves ouvertes"
  Cellar open-days
  (October 10) "Exposition des Champignons Sauvages"
  Wild mushroom exhibition
Sancerre: *(first weekend in May)* "Foire aux Fromages"
  Cheese Fair
  (Pentecost weekend) "Foire aux Vins"
  (last Sunday in October) "Foire aux Huîtres" Oyster Fair
Verdigny: *(last Sunday in July)* "Fêtes des Grappes Nouvelles"
  Grape Festival
Tigy: *(third Sunday in May)* "Foire aux Asperges"
  Asparagus Fair
Jargeau: *(end April)* "Concours des Vins de la Région Centre"
  Wine contest
  (second Sunday in June) "Foire aux Andouilles" Chitterling
  Sausage Fair
  (mid-October) "Foire aux Châtaignes" Chestnut Fair
Saint-Denis-de-l'Hôtel: *(May 30-31)* "Foire aux Fromages"
  Cheese Fair
Orléans: *(first week in May)* "Fête de Jeanne d'Arc" Joan of
  Arc Festival
Romorantin: *(late October)* "Journées Gastronomiques"
  Food Festival
Millançay: *(last weekend in September)* "Fête à la Citrouille"
  Pumpkin Festival
Mennetou-sur-Cher: *(first weekend in May)* "Foire aux
  Andouillettes" Chitterling Sausage Fair
Selles-sur-Cher: *(first Sunday after Easter)* "Foire aux Vins"
Saint-Aignan: *(last Saturday in October)* "Foire de St Simon"
Céré-la-Ronde: *(last Sunday in October)* "Foire aux Produits de
  Chèvre" Goat Products Fair

TOURAINE

Restaurants

BON LABOUREUR ET
CHÂTEAU
Chenonceaux
Tel 47 23 90 02
*Closed December 15 –
February 15*

LE MANOIR SAINT
THOMAS *
1 Mail Saint Thomas
Amboise Tel 47 57 22 52
*Closed January 15 – March 15
and Monday*

LE CHOISEUL
36 quai Charles-Guinot
Amboise Tel 47 30 45 45
*Closed December 8 –
January 18*

LES HAUTES ROCHES *
86 quai de la Loire
Rochecorbon
Tel 47 52 88 88
*Closed mid-January through
mid-March, Sunday evenings,
Monday except holidays*

AUBERGE DE LA
BRENNE
12 rue de la République
Neuillé-le-Lierre
Tel 47 52 95 05
*Closed Tuesday evenings,
Wednesday, mid-January
through February*

HOSTELLERIE DU
COQ-HARDI
rue Nationale
Monnaie Tel 47 56 10 17
*Closed Tuesday evenings and
Wednesday*

JEAN BARDET **
57 rue Groison
Tours Tel 47 41 41 11
*Closed Sunday evenings, Monday
from November 1 – April 1,
Monday lunchtimes in summer*

BISTROT DES HALLES
31 place Gastron-Paillhou
Tours Tel 47 61 54 93
Open daily

LE CORNEILLE
49 rue Colbert
Tours Tel 47 66 72 55
*Closed 1 week in February
and 3 weeks in August*

LE MOULIN FLEURI
route de Monts
Montbazon
Tel 47 26 01 12
*Closed October 15 – 31,
February, Monday except
holidays, Sunday evenings,
Monday during winter*

AUBERGE DU MOULIN
DES ROCHES
Saint-Épain
Sainte-Maure
Tel 47 65 80 47
Closed Monday, early January

DOMAINE DE
BEAUVOIS *
D49 Luynes
Tel 47 55 50 11
Closed January 5 – March 14

AUBERGE DU GRAND
VATEL
8 rue Brûlé
Vouvray Tel 47 52 70 32
*Closed Monday, first 2 weeks
Dec, first 2 weeks March*

LA CAVE MARTIN
La Vallée Coquette
Vouvray Tel 47 52 62 18
*Closed Sunday evenings,
Monday, and Christmas*

CHÂTEAU DE
ROCHECOTTE
Saint-Patrice
Tel 47 96 90 62
Closed February

LE GRAND MONARQUE
3 place de la République
Azay-le-Rideau
Tel 47 45 40 08
Open March 15 – November 6

L'AUTOMATE
GOURMAND
La Chapelle-Saint-Blaise
Azay-le-Rideau
Tel 47 45 39 07
*Closed March 1 – 20,
November 13 – 20, Tuesday*

AUBERGE DE L'ILE
L'Ile Bouchard
Tel 47 58 51 07
*Closed October, February,
Sunday evenings, Monday*

AU PLAISIR
GOURMAND *
quai Charles VII
Chinon Tel 47 93 20 48
*Closed Sunday evenings,
Monday, February*

HOSTELLERIE
GARGANTUA
73 rue Voltaire
Chinon Tel 47 93 04 71
*Closed Wednesday and
Thursday off-season,
November 15 through March*

CHÂTEAU DE MARÇAY
Marçay Tel 47 93 03 47
Closed January 10 – March 10

AUBERGE DE TOUVOIS
Bourgueil Tel 47 97 88 81
*Closed December 22 –
January 22, Monday*

GERMAIN
6 rue Alain Chartier
Bourgueil
Tel 47 97 72 22
*Closed October 1 – 21, Sunday
eves, Monday except holidays*

AUBERGE DU PORT
BOULET
Port Boulet
Chouzé-sur-Loire
Tel 47 95 15 92
Closed Sunday evenings

Markets

Amboise: *Friday, Sunday*
Vouvray: *Tuesday, Friday*
Loches: *Wednesday*
Tours: *daily, except Monday*

Joué-les-Tours: *Wednesday,
Thursday, Saturday, Sunday*
Montbazon: *Friday*
Veigné: *Friday*
Sainte-Maure-de-
Touraine: *Friday*
Luynes: *Saturday*
Langeais: *Sunday*
Azay-le-Rideau: *Wednesday*
Chinon: *Thursday, Saturday*
Richelieu: *Monday*
Bourgueil: *Tuesday, Sat*

Places of interest

DISTILLERIE "FRAISES
D'OR"
62 route de Tours
Chissay-en-Touraine
Tel 54 32 32 05
*Open Easter through end of
September, closed lunchtimes*

MUSÉE DES VINS DE
TOURAINE
16 rue Nationale
Tours Tel 47 61 07 93
*Closed Tuesday, holidays,
January and February*

L'ABBAYE DE
MARMOUTIER
17 quai Marmoutier
Tours Tel 47 05 58 08
Visit by appointment

CHÂTEAU DE
VILLANDRY
Villandry
Joué-lès-Tours
Tel 47 50 02 09
*Garden open daily. Château
closed mid-November
through mid-March*

MUSÉE DU TERROIR
(agriculture)
Villaines-les-Rochers
Azay-le-Rideau
Tel 47 45 43 08
Open Saturday and Sunday
afternoons in summer, or by
request

MUSÉE DU
BOUCHARDAIS
Ancienne Gare
L'Ile-Bouchard
Tel 47 58 56 65
Open Tuesday/Friday/Sunday
afternoons July 1 – August 31

Festivals/Fairs

Chenonceaux: (*third Sunday in July*) "Foire aux Boudins"
 Sausage Fair
Amboise: (*Easter Saturday*) "Foire aux Vins"
 (*15 August*) "Foire aux Vins"
 (*first Wednesday in September*) "Foire aux Melons" Melon
 Fair
Montreuil-en-Touraine: (*mid-September*) "Foire aux Pains"
 Bread Fair
Saint-Georges-sur-Cher: (*Easter weekend and Monday*) "Foire
 aux Vins"
Athée-sur-Cher: (*end March*) "Foire aux Andouillettes"
 Chitterling Sausage Fair
Bléré: (*second Friday in September*) "Foire aux Melons"
 Melon Fair
Vouvray: (*November 17*) "Dégustation de Vin Nouveau" Vin
 Nouveau tasting
 (*first Sunday of February*) "Foire aux Vins"
Preuilly-sur-Claise: (*early October*) "Foire aux Rillons" Potted
 Pork Fair
Tours: (*July 26*) "Foire à l'Ail et aux Échalotes" Garlic and
 Shallot Fair
Neuillé-Pont-Pierre: (*mid-May*) "Foire aux Fromages"
 Cheese Fair
Sainte-Maure: (*first Sunday in June*) "Foire aux Fromages"
 Cheese Fair
Lignières-de-Touraine: (*mid-November*) "Foire aux Pommes"
 Apple Fair
Azay-le-Rideau: (*end February*) "Foire aux Vins"
 (*first weekend in November*) "Foire aux Pommes" Apple Fair
Crouzilles: (*early December*) "Veillé aux Noix" Walnut Festival
Chinon: (*first weekend in March*) "Foire aux Vins"
 (*early August*) "Marché Médiéval" Medieval Feast
Bourgueil: (*last Tuesday in July*) "Foire à l'Ail" Garlic Fair
 (*first weekend in February*) "Foire aux Vins"

Specialties of the region

LE VIRAGE
GASTRONOMIQUE
(Charcuterie Hardouin)
25 route Nationale 152
Vouvray Tel 47 52 60 24
Open daily

LA PÂTISSERIE AND LA
CONFITERIE
TOURANGELLE
31 and 6 rue Nationale
Tours Tel 47 05 42 00
Open daily except Mondays,
closed lunchtimes

Vineyard Visiting

COMITÉ
INTERPROFESSIONNEL
DES VINS DE TOURAINE
(information on Touraine wines)
19 square Prosper-
Mérimée
Tours Tel 47 05 40 01

MAISON DES VINS
DE BLOIS
84 avenue de Verdun
Blois Tel 54 74 76 66
Closed lunchtimes and
Thursday

GASTON HUET
Le Haut Lieu
Vouvray Tel 47 52 78 87
Closed lunchtimes, Sundays
and Saints' Days

CAVES COOPERATIVES
DES PRODUCTEURS DES
GRAND VINS DE
VOUVRAY
Vallée Coquette
Vouvray Tel 47 52 75 03
Closed lunchtimes

MAISON AUDEBERT
ET FILS
20 avenue Jean Causeret
Bourgueil Tel 47 97 70 06
Closed lunchtimes, weekends,
August

COULY CAVES
12 rue Diderot
Chinon Tel 47 93 05 84
Closed lunchtimes, Saturday
afternoons, Sundays, holidays

ANJOU

Restaurants

AUBERGE DE L'ABBAYE
8 avenue des Roches
Fontevraud-l'Abbaye
Tel 41 51 71 04
Closed October 6 – 29, Tuesday
evenings, Wednesday

LA LICORNE *
31 rue Robert-d'Arbrissel
Fontevraud-l'Abbaye
Tel 41 51 72 49
Closed January and February,
Sunday evenings, Monday

LE CHAPY
Allonnes Tel 41 52 02 63
Closed Monday/Tuesday/
Wednesday/Sunday evenings

L'ESCARGOT
30 rue Maréchal LeClerc
Saumur Tel 41 51 20 88
Closed January, Wednesday

LES MENÉSTRALS
11 rue Raspail
Saumur Tel 41 67 71 10
Closed Sunday, Monday, last
week in December

LE PRIEURÉ
Chênehutte-les-Tuffeaux
nr. Saumur Tel 41 67 90 14
Closed January and February,
open all week

AUBERGE JEANNE
DE LAVAL *
54 rue Nationale
Les Rosiers-sur-Loire
Tel 41 51 80 17
Closed January 8 –
February 17, Mondays
except holidays

PAVILLON PAUL
LE QUÉRÉ
3 boulevard Foch
Angers Tel 41 20 00 20
Open daily all year

LA SALAMANDRE
1 boulevard Maréchal-
Foch
Angers Tel 41 88 99 55
Closed Sunday

LA PETIT MÂCHON
43 rue Bressigny
Angers Tel 41 86 01 13
Closed Saturday lunchtimes,
Sunday, August

AUBERGE D'EVENTARD
route de Paris
Saint-Sylvain-d'Anjou
Tel 41 43 74 25
Closed Sunday evenings,
Monday, first 2 weeks Feb

LE CLAFOUTIS
route de Paris
Saint-Sylvain-d'Anjou
Tel 41 43 84 71
Closed Tuesday evenings,
Wednesday, Sunday

LE RELAIS DE
BONNEZEAUX
Thouarcé Tel 41 54 08 33
Closed Wednesday, second half
December, second week Feb

NOTRE DAME
place de l'Église
Béhuard
Saint-Georges-sur-Loire
Tel 41 72 20 17
Closed Wednesday

Markets

Fontevraud-l'Abbaye:
  Wednesday
Saumur: *Tuesday,*
  Wednesday, Thursday, Sat
Gennes: *Tuesday*
Les Rosiers: *Monday*
Baugé: *Monday*
Beaufort-en-Vallée:
  Wednesday
Mazé: *Friday*
Thouarcé: *Tuesday*
Angers: *daily*
Saint-Sylvain-d'Anjou:
  Sunday
Châteauneuf-sur-Sarthe:
  Friday

Rochefort-sur-Loire:
  Wednesday
Saint-Georges-sur-Loire:
  Thursday
Montjean-sur-Loire:
  Thursday
Cholet: *Tuesday, Wednesday,*
  Thursday, Saturday

Places of interest

ABBAYE DE
FONTEVRAUD
Fontevraud-l'Abbaye
Tel 41 51 71 41
Closed 1 – 11 November,
1 January, 1 May

MUSÉE DU
CHAMPIGNON
La Houssay
St-Hilaire-St-Florent
Saumur Tel 41 50 31 55

CHÂTEAU DE
MONTGEOFFROY
Mazé Tel 41 80 60 02
Open all year

VILLAGE
TROGLODYTIQUE DE
ROCHEMENIER
Louresse-Rochemenier
Doué-la-Fontaine
Tel 41 59 18 15
Open 1 April – 15 November

COINTREAU
rue de la Croix Blanche
ZI Saint-Barthélémy
(industrial park)
Saint-Barthélémy-d'Anjou
Tel 41 43 25 21
Open daily by appointment

MUSÉE DE LA VIGNE ET
DU VIN D'ANJOU
place des Vignerons
Saint-Lambert-du-Lattay
Tel 41 78 42 75
Closed 1 November –
31 March

MUSÉE DES VIEUX
MÉTIERS
Saint-Laurent-de-la-Plaine
Chalonnes-sur-Loire
Tel 41 78 24 08
Closed 1 November – 1 April

Specialties of the region

LE VAL HULIN
(Pommes Tapées)
Turquant
nr. Saumur Tel 41 51 48 30
Open daily June through
September, call for rest of year

LES CAVES DE MARSON
(Fouaces)
Marson
nr. Saumur Tel 41 67 10 12

HUILERIE CROIX VERTE
29 rue Bouju
St-Lambert-des-Levées
Tel 41 67 43 00

Vineyard visiting

MAISON DES VINS
DE L'ANJOU
(information center for Anjou
and Saumur wines)
5 bis place Kennedy
Angers Tel 41 88 81 13

MAISON DES VINS
DE SAUMUR
(information center for Saumur
wine producers)
25 rue Beaurepaire
Saumur Tel 41 51 16 40

COULÉE DE SERRANT
Château Roche aux
Moines Tel 41 72 22 32
Closed Sunday and holidays

GRATIEN-MEYER
rue Beaulieu
Saumur Tel 41 51 01 54
Open daily all year

BUVET LADUBAY
rue de l'Abbaye
St-Hilaire-St-Florent
Saumur Tel 41 50 11 12
Open daily all year

Festivals/Fairs

Saumur: *(date to be decided)* "Foire du Vin" Wine weekend
Villebernier: *(last weekend in May)* "Fête des Fraises" Strawberry Festival
Chacé: *(first weekend in September)* "Foire au Champigny" Champigny Wine Fair
Souzay-Champigny: *(June)* "Fête à la Friture" Deep-Fried Fish Festival
Vernoil: *(May)* "Foire au Asperges" Asparagus Fair
Mouliherne: *(October 19-20)* "Foire aux Pommes" Apple Fair
Beauné: *(first Saturday in September)* "Foire aux Rillauds" Potted Pork Fair
Coutures: *(third weekend in September)* "Foire aux Artichauts" Artichoke Fair
Saint-Gemmes-sur-Loire: *(third weekend in June)* "Fête à la Tomate" Tomato Fair
Brissac-Quincé: *(November 16)* "Concours d'Anjou Rouge" Red Anjou competition
  (end September) "Foire aux Aulx" Garlic Fair
Angers: *(January)* "Foire au Miel" Honey Fair
Vauchrétien: *(last weekend in July)* "Foire aux Lumas" Snail Fair
Thouarcé: *(first Sunday in June)* "Foires aux Vins et aux Fromages" Wine and Cheese Fair
Saint-Aubin-de-Luigné: *(third weekend in July)* "Fête aux Vins"
Saint-Lambert-du-Lattay: *(second Sunday in July)* "Fête à la Vinée" Coteaux-du-Layon wine competition
La Poueze: *(Saturday closest to August 24)* "Foire aux Melons" Melon Fair
Chalonnes-sur-Loire: *(last weekend in February)* "Foire aux Vins" *(last weekend in August)* "Foire aux Melons" Melon Fair

PAYS NANTAIS

Restaurants

LES JARDINS DE LA FORGE *
1 bis place Piliers
Champtoceaux
Tel 40 83 56 23
Closed October 8 – 23, Sunday and Tuesday evenings, Wednesday

BEAU RIVAGE
Clermont-sur-Loire
Le Cellier Tel 40 25 46 40
Closed Sunday evenings, Monday, second half of August

LE ROSERARIE
3 avenue de la Gare
Mauves-sur-Loire
Tel 40 25 50 21
Closed Tuesday

CLÉMENCE
La Chebuette
Saint Julien de Concelles
Tel 40 54 10 18
Closed first 3 weeks of December, Sunday evenings, Monday

MON RÊVE
route des Bords de Loire
Basse-Goulaine
Tel 40 03 55 50
Closed November, February, Tuesday evenings, Wednesday

LE COLVERT
14 rue Armand-Brossard
Nantes Tel 40 48 20 02
Closed Sunday

LES MARAÎCHERS
21 rue Fouré
(Champ de Mars)
Nantes Tel 40 47 06 51

VIÉ
quai de l'Erdre
Sucé-sur-Erdre
Tel 40 77 70 06
Closed first half of January, Sunday evenings

LA CHÂTAIGNERAIE **
156 route Carquefou
Sucé-sur-Erdre
Tel 40 77 90 95
Closed July 29 – August 12, January, Monday, Sunday evenings

LES VOYAGEURS
place de l'Eglise
Paulx Tel 40 26 02 26
Closed January 2 – 8, September 10 – 23, Sunday evenings, Monday

DOMAINE D'ORVAULT *
Chemin des Marais du Cens
Orvault (n. of Nantes)
Tel 40 76 84 02
Closed Monday lunchtimes, February

MANOIR DE LA COMÈTE
21 rue de la Libération
St-Sébastien (s. of Nantes)
Tel 40 34 15 93
Closed first week of January and first 2 weeks of August, Sunday

Markets

Ancenis: Thursday
Vallet: *Sunday*
Basse-Goulaine: *Wednesday*
Haute-Goulaine: *Tuesday*
Saint-Sébastien-sur-Loire: *Tuesday, Thursday, Friday*
Nantes: *daily (Saturday is best)*
Carquefou: *Thursday*
La Chapelle-sur-Erdre: *Wednesday, Friday, Sunday*
Sucé-sur-Erdre: *Tuesday*
Nort-sur-Erdre: *Tuesday, Friday*
Orvault: *Friday*
Bourgneuf-en-Retz: *Saturday*
Le Croisic: *Thursday*

Places of interest

MUSÉE PIERRE-ABÉLARD
Le Pallet
Vallet Tel 40 26 42 15
Closed weekdays except holidays and closed November 1 through Easter

MUSÉE D'ARTS POPULAIRES DE BRETAGNE
Château des Ducs de Bretagne
Nantes Tel 40 47 02 42
Closed Tuesday, holidays

MUSÉE DE PAYS DE RETZ
Bourgneuf
Tel 40 21 40 83
Closed December through Easter

Specialties of the region

MICHEL HOYET
(L'Hermine d'Or)
19 rue Paul-Bellamy
Nantes Tel 40 48 15 20
Closed October 1 – April 31, Sunday, Monday

Vineyard Visiting

LOUIS MÉTAIREAU
La Févrie
Maisdon-sur-Sèvre
Tel 40 54 81 92
Open all year by appointment

Festivals/Fairs

Vallet: (March 14-16) "Foire aux Vins"
Nantes: (mid-October) "Fête des Châtaignes et du Vin" Chestnut and Wine Festival
Nozay: (early October) "Fête des Boudins" Sausage Festival
Saint-Nazaire: (15 September) "Foire aux Oignons" Onion Fair

CHÂTEAU DE GOULAINE
Haute-Goulaine
Tel 40 54 91 42
Closed Tuesday afternoons

SAUVION ET FILS
Château de Cléray
Vallet Tel 40 36 22 55
Open weekdays Easter – end of September

MAISON DES VINS
Belle rue
La Haie-Fouassière
nr. Nantes
Tel 40 36 90 10

LIST OF RECIPES

INDEX

ACKNOWLEDGMENTS

AUTHOR'S ACKNOWLEDGMENTS

Many people have helped me during the life of this book, and to all of them I am sincerely grateful. There were many formal and pre-arranged introductions, but while I was doing "on the ground" research, I was helped spontaneously so often that people's generosity with their time, and money, began to cease to surprise me. The list of storekeepers, stall holders, restaurateurs, chefs, cooks, friends, and relatives of contacts of mine, and people I just happened to come across, is too long to include everyone. Where possible I have mentioned them in the book, but to all the others who are not included there or below and to anyone else who has helped me, "Thank you very much."

M. & Mme Benoist, Château du Plessis; M. & Mme Berthoumier, St-Avertin, near Tours; Brittany Ferries; Mme Cabanes, Relais & Châteaux, Paris; Philip Doumerc, Le Prieuré, Chenehutte-les-Tuffeaux; Food & Wine From France; Didier Garnier, St Quentin Group, London; Mme Garnier, Angers; M. & Mme Goupil de Bouillé, Châteaux de Reaux; Martin Hollis and all the staff at World Wide Wine Tours; Louis Métaireau; P & O Ferries; Alison Cryer at Representation Plus; Michel Sébéo, St-Aignan; Alain Seydoux, Gratien & Meyer, Saumur; M. Taupin, Domaine du Beauvois, Luynes;

M. & Mme de Valbray, Château des Briotieres; Comte and Comtesse de Voguë, Château de la Verrerie.

Finally, I thank my editor, Sarah Pearce, for her hard work, efficiency, and understanding.

RESEARCHER'S ACKNOWLEDGMENTS

Sally Anne Scott would like to thank all the chefs and restaurateurs who gave so much of their time to the book, particularly those who sadly could not be featured.

PUBLISHER'S ACKNOWLEDGMENTS

Studio photography
(pages **23, 29, 50-1, 54, 78-9, 87, 88-9, 113, 139, 145**)
Home Economist   Meg Jansz
Photographer's assistant   Leonor Silva

Visitors' Guide research   *Index*
Jane Sigal   Karin Woodruff